Consciousness Is All There Is

GOD IS CONSCIOUSNESS

Hadsy Simon

Copyright © 2014 Hadsy Simon
All rights reserved.

ISBN: 1500110752
ISBN 13: 9781500110758
Library of Congress Control Number: 2014910519
CreateSpace Independent Publishing Platform
North Charleston, South Carolina

CONTENTS

Chapter 1   Consciousness, God, and the Universe 1

Chapter 2   Your Belief System 16

Chapter 3   Emotions 24

Chapter 4   What is Reality 42

Chapter 5   Consciousness 53

Chapter 6   A new world 63

I dedicate this book with love to my children
Marlon, Heidy, Edward, and Michael.

I am very grateful to my partner
Karine de Jongh,
for the loving care she has offered me
during all the years we have been together.

PREFACE

We are living in a world of turmoil agitated by economic crises, political and religious conflicts, and social commotions. After the end of World War I and II, in which an estimated sixty-five million people were killed and more than 120 million wounded, we might have thought that we were going to enjoy a long-lasting peace, but nothing was further from the truth. From 1945, the end of WW II, to 2013, the time of this writing, there have been some 250 wars around the world, resulting in over fifty million people killed and countless millions injured and made homeless.

On top of these wars, an increase of natural disasters around the world is taking a toll. It also looks as if we cannot halt the exploitation and contamination of nature. The killing and extinction of animal species are rising. Further, corruption is present in all our institutions, and man seems to be more egocentric than ever.

My writing is a reflection on what I think is our true nature and on the need for each of us to take direct responsibility for the proper changes to save planet Earth. It is time to supplant myths, surpass ego trips, substitute Consciousness for religious gods, devote more time in spiritual practices, and spend more time in reading and understanding how each of us can influence the conservation of planet Earth and the uplifting of humanity. We are not here just to wage wars, exploit nature, see others starve, and succumb to our cravings. We are spiritual beings, and it is time for us to accomplish much more in the direction of peace and love; all we need is the attitude.

My writing has been kept simple; at the end of the book I provide a list of books, and I hope the reader will explore some of them. I am convinced that by much reading we can become wiser in the spiritual sense of the word and that we thus can adopt the attitude of striving for a world of more peace and understanding, beginning with ourselves.

This book was published with the monetary help of my children, Marlon Simon, Heidy Simon, Edward Simon, and Michael Simon, and my nephew Michel Simon. Thank you all so very much.

I have always liked reading and have read numerous books; for the past thirty years the idea of writing a book myself has been hovering. Then one day my son Edward said, "Dad, why don't you write a book?" That was it; the idea descended! Here is the book!

Hadsy Simon

Chapter 1

CONSCIOUSNESS, GOD, AND THE UNIVERSE

Imagine nothing, absolutely nothing, no universe, no you, no me. Can something come out of nothing? Where did what we call God come from? Where did consciousness come from? Where did the universe come from? Where did the laws governing nature come from? Let us try to give an answer to these questions.

Before I go on, let me state that when I use the word *God*, I do not refer to a god with human attributes like the gods of religions with their punishments, hell, and wars; such gods do not exist.

Let us start with this question: Where did God come from? If we say that God has been created by another god, we will promptly ask: And who created that other god? It will easily be seen that this questioning will go on ad infinitum. So, let's accept for now that God was not created. He has always been. God is eternal. He had no beginning, and He will have no end.

Does this mean that God originated out of nothing? When I say nothing, I mean absolutely nothing. But, what is "nothing"? It could be argued that "nothing" is "something"—it is nothingness. We then ask, did God originate out of nothing? The answer is no, God did not **originate** out of nothing. **God is nothingness.** He did not originate. God has always been and will always be; God is eternal besides being infinite.

What is God? I could not ask this question or any other question if I were not conscious; to consider anything, study anything, or know anything, I must be conscious. Nothing in the universe would make any sense if I were not conscious. I would not be aware that I exist if I were not conscious, and the same goes for every being. This also applies to God. God is not only conscious. **God is Consciousness.** So, nothingness, God, and Consciousness are the very same "thing" Such an enigmatic and spiritual entity is at the source of all research and knowledge.

Now, how does God become conscious, and what does God become conscious of? God is not a person, It is not a thing, not an entity. You may call it God, It, He, She, whatever; It does not feel offended by the name. Being absolute and infinite, God cannot experience Itself, there is nothing to experience, It is the sole existence. To undergo an experience, we need at least two beings like an "I" and a "you." So, God decides to "split" Itself in an infinite number of conscious Selves. But to split Itself would mean to become finite, and, besides, a space would be created between the split Selves of God. None of this could be. God in Its infinite nature cannot become finite, and space cannot be created in infinity. Space does not exist. God is one, absolute, infinite, and eternal. It is nondual, **nothing else exists in the universe, absolutely nothing else!**

Now, let us ask: where did Consciousness come from? Consciousness and God are the very same "thing." We, as conscious beings, consider God to be something or someone separate from us. But this is an illusion.

Now, let us consider this question: where did Consciousness and matter come from? To know that you are conscious, you have to become aware of something, and that something is matter. Matter is an **illusory** creation of Consciousness. God and Consciousness are the very same "thing"—they are ONE and this Oneness creates matter to become aware of Its own existence and to experience Itself. So, **the sole existence is and remains God-Consciousness,** and the laws governing the universe are **inherent** in matter; you need the laws for the forthcoming of matter in an orderly manner, and you need matter to prove the existence of the laws. So, the only existence is **God-Consciousness, w**e are all God-Consciousness. Every human being, every animal, every plant, all minerals, the whole infinite universe— all is God-Consciousness. That is why, as the most developed conscious being, we, as human beings, can create whatever we want, and **we do create** whatever we want. More on this in a later chapter.

But, how then did that first thing or being we call God come about, where did it come from, how could it be without a cause? We do not know the answer to these questions, but faced with such mysterious, unfathomable issue, we can only accept the explanation of God as necessary. Necessary, in philosophy, means something that we must accept as having no cause, it has been there all the time. Necessary is something that is primordial, something that has always been, and once it is, there is no need for a second necessary thing. Anything that comes afterward must have originated from the first thing and is that first thing. The necessary thing or entity is eternal and infinite. There is no duality.

God is not right, God is not wrong, God is not good, God is not bad. You cannot use any adjective to describe or evaluate God. God is not even perfect;

God is, period! All evaluations, like right and wrong, by a Conscious Being, are expressions of the Belief System of that being. A Conscious Being, or simply Consciousness, hides or obscures Its absolute knowledge behind a Belief System to be able to experience the world. We will explain Belief System in Chapter 2.

To know that something exists we need a subject and an object. The subject is the observer, the one that is going to analyze an object, and the object is the one being observed, the one being analyzed. To observe and analyze you need to be conscious, that is, you need Consciousness. Now, the object being analyzed happens to be "made out" of Consciousness because Consciousness is all that exists. Thus, Consciousness is actually subject and object at the same time; the observer becomes the observed. This is what makes the study of Consciousness so difficult because the one that observes is the one being observed. I repeat: To experience you need at least "two". You need an "I" and a "you," and God, being the sole existence, cannot experience Itself. That is the reason why It had to "split" Itself in a "you" and a "me" and in infinite other beings of the animal, plant, and mineral world. But also this is an enigma because God is infinite and if God were to split Itself It would become "finite," and this would be a contradiction. Besides, when you split something, you create space in between the thing being split, and space does not exist in infinity. So, the splitting of God is an illusion, an illusion created by Itself. The whole universe is nondual. There exists only one eternal and infinite entity: God-Consciousness.

In religion we address ourselves to a God outside of us. It is in our Belief System that God must be someone separated from us. In John 10:30 Jesus said, "The Father and I are one"; the truth is, we are all one with the Father. Jesus never considered himself as special and different. In John 10:34 Jesus said, "You are Gods."

So, the very first thing or entity was necessary. It has always existed, it exists now, and it will always exist; this first thing is what we call God. Actually, God was not the "first" thing either because there never was a second thing. God was, period. Everything that came along after the "first thing" must have originated from It and is inherent in It; nothing exists separate from It. **Everything is a manifestations of It and in It.**

Let's cleanse God of some misunderstandings. God is not an individual. He (or she) is not a person. He is not standing somewhere in a place called heaven. He does not punish or reward anybody. We, human beings, have invented God. We have made him just as we are, and we have described him in some books called scriptures, such as the Bible and the Koran. And why did we do this? Because we ourselves are that way. We struggle all the time with hate, anger, sadness, jealousy, love, and so on, **so we invented a god to our image and likeness.** These books have been written by men, not by God, and neither were they inspired by God. To say that *God is an individual with human attributes* is perhaps the myth that has done most harm to humans.

Why did we invent God as something outside of ourselves, something out there in heaven? First we have to ask ourselves why we invented God in the first place. Primitive humans saw and were overwhelmed by natural forces such as lightning, thunder, rain, volcanoes, earthquakes, storms, and floods. Not being able to explain these phenomena, which had a power far beyond human intervention, they ascribed them to a superhuman creature. Because this power manifested in the "outside world," they also thought of this creature as if it existed in the outside world, as if in the clouds, in a heaven, or wherever. Different tribes gave different names to this sort of superpower, and thousands of years later, names such as God, Allah, Yahweh, Vishnu, and others were invented. But these names are just words. They are metaphors, and they do not say anything about the attributes or nature of a being called God, Allah, or whatever.

The institutions that have created the most misunderstanding around God are religions. They invented a vengeful God, a God that punishes some and rewards others. The truth is He does not punish or reward. In a strict sense, there is no punishment or reward in the universe. You could say that we "punish" and "reward" ourselves. When you do something wrong and you walk around with the unpleasant feeling of resentment, that is your "punishment." When you make someone happy with your acts and you walk around with a feeling of contentment, that is your "reward." There are continuously an infinite number of happenings in the universe, and none of them is either right or wrong, good or bad. They just happen; they just are. It is our Belief System that evaluates them as right or wrong, good or bad. Absolute right and absolute wrong do not exist, period! Consciousness-God experiences Itself through all these acts.

But why do we insist in the existence of God outside of us? We insist because, as I said before, as primitive humans, we created God as the being responsible for all those things that came out of the sky, sea, and earth that we could not understand; it was perhaps one of the first beliefs that formed our Belief System. After that, there were men called priests who perpetuated those beliefs in us. Furthermore, it is comfortable to blame someone, like God, for all the pain we derive from our irresponsible behavior or from misfortunes that strike us.

Imagine our galaxy, the Milky Way. It contains **a hundred billion stars**, and it forms part of another **nineteen galaxies, each with a hundred billion stars** of its own. Beyond this, as far as astronomers can see, there are **another hundred billion galaxies**, each with, again, **a hundred billion stars**. Now, do you, my dear reader, sincerely believe that the originator of this infinite universe will grant you one lifetime and then will punish you for eternity for having robbed, or killed, or not gone to church on Sunday, or what have you? **This is just an absurd, silly fairy tale.**

Now, as mysterious as the origin of God is the origin of Consciousness. Some scientists believe that Consciousness is an epiphenomenon of the processes of the brain—that is, it comes about as a result of the functioning of the brain. But this is not so because something totally nonmaterial, something totally nonenergetic, cannot result from something completely material as the brain. Consciousness possesses properties far beyond any property ascribed to material objects.

Consciousness is indispensable to become aware of the universe. There cannot be a universe if nobody is aware of it; it makes no sense. Let me say it another way: suppose you create something, but you are not aware you created it. You cannot see your creation; you cannot hear it, feel it, smell it, or taste it. How do you know you created it? What sense does it make? You are not aware of your creation, and that is impossible; you cannot create and not be aware of what you created because **to create you have to be conscious**, and if you are conscious you are aware (conscious) of your creation. **Consciousness creates and sustains creation.**

It has been shown in quantum mechanics that a subatomic particle does not exist as long as the physicist does not intend to find it; it is the consciousness of the physicist that "collapses the probability wave" and brings the particle into existence. This is also applicable to the macro world; everything in the macro world is created by conscious human beings—a table, an airplane, a sheet of paper, everything. An object may have been built by a robot, but the robot does this by a built-in program installed by conscious human beings. Consciousness is involved directly in everything in the universe. The laws of physics, biology, and so on are manifestations of Consciousness. As an example, if under the proper circumstances of pressure, temperature, and magnetic field, you bring together two atoms of hydrogen and one atom of oxygen, you will **always** get water. This is a manifestation of Consciousness through Its laws of nature, and this applies to the whole universe.

The laws of nature are unconditionally and inherently bonded to their material manifestations; they are one and the very same manifestation. Miracles do not exist. A "miracle" is a manifestation of a law of nature for which we do not yet have an adequate explanation.

But what is Consciousness? We do not know. We do know that you must be conscious to create, that all creation emerges from Consciousness, and that **the Universal Consciousness, the Primordial Consciousness, is what we call God. GOD IS CONSCIOUSNESS AND CONSCIOUSNESS IS GOD.**

Now, let us go back to this Primordial Universal Consciousness. Can this Universal Consciousness have any experience? The answer is no, Universal

Consciousness cannot have an experience, It needs something or someone besides Itself to have an experience with. So, It "splits" Itself in multiple "Is." As spiritual evolution goes on, there comes a moment when, in human beings, each "I" becomes conscious of him- or herself. When this happens, the self-conscious "I" now considers him- or herself as unique, and this "I"—a man or a woman—will identify a "different" "I" as a "you." So one becomes two, and separation and distance have taken place. The reaction of each "I" is "You are not me, I cannot trust you," and so FEAR makes its entrance in the human kingdom; **fear is at the basis of all our sufferings**.

The sole Universal Consciousness one day emitted an infinite number of "sparks" of Itself; these "sparks" became the infinite number of Conscious Beings that exist in the universe—that is, all human beings, all animals, all plants, all minerals, and all atomic and subatomic particles. Now, why did Universal-Consciousness emit sparks of Itself? We do not know, but we suppose it must have been because It had nothing to be conscious about. God wanted to experience Itself and It does this through the infinite experiences of all Conscious Beings. I will repeat: Primordial Universal Consciousness, **being the only entity that exists**, has nothing to be conscious of. It cannot be conscious of Itself and experience Itself while being the only existence. So, It made an "image" of Itself. Actually It made infinite "images" of Itself, and these images are all human beings, animals, plants, and minerals.

At the moment of birth, a human being is engulfed by a Belief System and forgets his source of emergence. By spiritual doctrines, he now has to develop and grow to recognize his God-Nature. This is the metaphor of Adam and Eve: they wanted to become God, but by wanting to become God, they negated their God-Nature. Adam and Eve are you and me, all human beings. We first forget that we are God, we negate our God-Nature; then, obscured by our material body and our Belief System, we go through numerous incarnations and infinite experiences, and so God experiences Itself through us, or actually **as us. We are God, everything is a form of God.** The whole universe is God, only God exists. Each "spark" of God experiences Itself until It becomes conscious of Its true nature; these are the enlightened masters, like, for example, Jesus or Buddha. They do not have to incarnate any longer; they lose their human identity and are absorbed in the Universal Consciousness.

So, first we have Universal Consciousness; there is nothing else other than It. Universal Consciousness generates an intention to create. The intention is surrounded by the laws of creation. Then the creation manifests and becomes conscious-material. Then the conscious-material becomes aware of itself as a "separate entity," as an obscured, enclosed individual. The enclosed individual is obscured by his or her Belief System; now he or she must strive to realize he or she is Absolute Consciousness. It is this striving with all its pain and pleasure that we call life. The suffering ends when you become enlightened and you become one with It, your true nature.

It may be that you want to become enlightened but do not want to lose your identity, your individuality. You strive to attain more riches, more power, or a larger ego, but to become enlightened you have to detach from all these. You are so identified with your ego that to lose it is like "dying," and who wants to die? Nobody. We are all afraid of the unknown act of "dying." And so you live in anguish. But the bottom line is that to return to your true nature, you must let go of this material illusion, and sooner or later we will all become enlightened. That is the ultimate purpose of life. **Actually, we are all already enlightened, because we all are God**, but we do not realize this because we are enclosed in this container called a body, and besides that, we are engulfed by a Belief System that enables us to experience all pain and pleasure.

So, **every conscious being is God**, and there is a degree of Consciousness in everything. There is a degree of Consciousness in **all atoms, all subatomic particles, and all minerals, plants, and animals. They all have a degree of Consciousness appropriate to their form and function. We are Consciousness-God, and so is everything.** Consciousness-God manifests and experiences Itself through all beings, through everything in the universe. Whatever we perceive, **It** is perceiving; whatever we experience, **It** is experiencing; whatever we feel, **It** is feeling. **Consciousness-God experiences Itself through you and me, through every animal, through every plant, through every mineral, through the whole universe.**

When studying something, you have a subject (the one doing the study) and an object (what is being studied). The study of Consciousness is very complicated and profound because Consciousness is both subject and object at the same time. When you study the object Consciousness, the one doing the study is you, a conscious subject, so you are actually studying yourself. You have to be conscious to do the study. The same applies to Consciousness-God. Consciousness-God is conscious, and you are conscious. So, when the you-**Consciousness** is studying God-**Consciousness**, you are studying yourself. Again, the same applies when you try to study yourself. The you-Consciousness is studying the you-Consciousness. Therefore, the only way to understand Consciousness is by **becoming conscious that you are Consciousness**. By becoming absolutely conscious that you are God-Consciousness, you conceive the God-nature in you. You can do this by spiritual studies and exercises.

You become enlightened. You have reached the ultimate step of spiritual evolution. You have liberated yourself, and you are now free from all "I," "me," "ego," "self," and "suffering." You return to Universal Consciousness.

What Is the Purpose of Life?

What could be the purpose of life if Universal Consciousness is all there is in the universe? You could say that there is no purpose, which is a desired result. Actually, God-Consciousness cannot desire. It has, or rather, It *is* everything; there is nothing to be desired. Besides, every outcome already exists in God-Consciousness. It encompasses everything. There is nothing to be added or to be subtracted in the universe. **All creation is already complete in this very moment, *now*.**

It is all a game, it is a play. We could say that **the purpose of life is God-Consciousness experiencing Itself**. It does this through Its infinite "parts": you, me, and the infinite beings in the universe. At every billionth of a second, there are infinite beings experiencing pleasure and pain. When you sum all the pleasures and all the pains in the universe, you get zero. (For example: $-10 + 10 = 0$.) This is a paradox: **It experiences without experiencing.**

Universal-God-Consciousness can experience only through us; as It covers Itself-Us in a Belief-Emotional-System, experiencing becomes possible. The Universal-God-Consciousness Itself cannot experience because there is nothing to experience; everything is and is not in It. By enclosing Itself in us, by enclosing Itself in a Belief-Emotional-System, by allowing separateness, by obscuring Its true nature in us, animals, plants, and minerals, experience becomes possible.

So, God-Consciousness experiences your joy and your pain, my joy and my pain, everybody's joy and everybody's pain. God-Consciousness experiences the pain of the whale while it is being harpooned, and It experiences the harshness of the killers. It experiences the fear of the elephant and the gorilla being chased and the cruelty of the poachers. It experiences the anguish of a dying man, the madness of a Hitler, the shame and filth of a little girl being abused and the sickness of the perpetrator. It experiences the anguish, the fear, and the hate of every soldier on the battlefield. It experiences the fury of the wounded lion. It experiences the confusion of the newborn baby. It experiences the stress of the fell tree. It feels the joy of the couple in love, the joy of the mother embracing her newborn baby. It experiences every single sensation and event there is to be experienced in the whole universe.

Actually, emotions do not exist by themselves; you must evaluate and interpret an experience through your Belief System in order to feel an emotion. An emotion cannot and does not arise if you do not evaluate an event; try to feel hate, or jealousy, or whatever emotion without thinking of an event that is taking place, has taken place, or will be taking place. You just cannot feel the emotion. An emotion is not a feeling that exists by itself. An event must happen first, and the event should be interpreted by a conscious being, and the interpretation must be appraised by a Belief System. Universal Consciousness (God) cannot do this because it has no Belief System of Itself. For emotions to exist, a material body must be created. This material body must be imbued by a Belief System through which events and feelings will be evaluated, and then you can originate an emotion. More on this in Chapter 3.

This is a participatory universe; we are all cocreators. It is an information universe; information takes place instantaneously every billionth of a second. There is no time and no space. The whole universe is filled with Universal Consciousness. You can learn more on this in the concepts of quantum mechanics.

Universal Consciousness is infinite. It is everywhere. There is not one billionth of a millimeter where It is not. The whole infinite universe is God—inside and outside of every human, animal, plant, and mineral; inside and outside of every molecule, atom, and subatomic particle; in all vacuum, in all fields, in light.

Now, can you exist as a finite being in this infinite universe? The answer is no, you do not exist as a finite being. If you were finite, then you would interrupt and break the infiniteness of Universal Consciousness, which would then also become finite. You are not finite. You are infinite. You are one with Universal Consciousness; you are OMNIPRESENT with Universal Consciousness; you are everywhere in every moment. **YOU AND GOD ARE ONE, YOU ARE GOD, GOD IS YOU!** Omnipresent means present everywhere at the same time. You-God is infinite; infinite means unbounded, unlimited. In infiniteness there is no space, and if there is no space then there is no time. God is everywhere in every moment;

you are everywhere in every moment; everywhere is **HERE,** and every moment is **NOW.** There is no past. Past exists only as a memory. There is no future; future exists only as an aspiration.

Creation is complete. There is nothing more to be created, and there is nothing missing. There is no past and no future. The whole creation is happening **now,** and it happens **here.** There is nowhere else.

The universe is infinite. There is not one trillionth of a millimeter empty; everywhere is filled with Consciousness. Time does not exist; everything happens instantaneously. It is in our Belief System that, for convenience purposes, we created terms such as "there" and "later."

In this infinite and timeless universe, **YOU ARE ME, I AM YOU, WE ARE ONE. WE ARE CONSCIOUSNESS, WE ARE GOD.**

> The whole universe is a play.
> The author of the play is God-Consciousness.
> The producer is God-Consciousness.
> The director is God-Consciousness.
> The actors are God-Consciousness.
> The audience is God-Consciousness.
> The play is experienced by God-Consciousness.
> There is nothing else besides God-Consciousness, It is creating the play
> **right here and right now.**

Chapter 2

YOUR BELIEF SYSTEM

The play is about to begin; a spark of Universal Consciousness is about to enter the material world. Consciousness cannot enter in direct contact with matter. It needs an intermediate substance between Itself and matter. Matter and the intermediate substance are all a creation of Consciousness Itself. Let's call the intermediate state life force, or soul. An analogy is to be found in electricity. The positive pole cannot enter in direct contact with the negative pole, or a short circuit will occur; a resistance has to be put in between. By comparison, matter is the negative pole, the soul is the resistance, and Consciousness is the positive pole. Experience is now going to take place—experience of pain, pleasure, hate, love, compassion, jealousy, and all the feelings and emotions a human being can go through. Consciousness, in Its pure state, cannot have these experiences; It must cover up Itself in the "limitations" of the soul and the Belief System. Emotions and feelings cannot take place in the universe. They must be created in a system, a system composed of beliefs, the immune system, the brain, and the soul; Consciousness is there just to interpret and feel them.

Consciousness is infinite. In infiniteness no experience can take place. For experience to take place you need a "subject" and an "object," an "I" and a "you," a "perpetrator" and a "victim." They both are "one"; they both are Universal God. Besides, for all those experiences to happen, you need space and time, and in infinity there is no space and no time. You create space and time in your Belief System.

The Belief System is a series of beliefs that human beings acquire when he enter this world. When children are born, they live often in the spiritual world up to the age of about six years. They will be hearing sounds and seeing images of disincarnated spirits; spirits are Consciousnesses that may not be incarnated at that time. The infant's brain, in this stage, will be functioning in alpha (7.5–14 Hz), which is the same brain wave one has when under hypnosis. (Normally adults' brain waves function in beta, 14–40 Hz.) For this reason, children will readily accept instructions given to them by their parents, the same as a person under hypnosis accepts the instructions given by the hypnotist.

In hypnosis your Conscious mind is bypassed and suggestions are given to your Sub-Conscious mind. According to some studies, your Sub-Conscious mind can process four hundred billion bits of information per second while the Conscious mind can process only two thousand bits per second. Why is this? First, remember that actually the Sub-Conscious and the Conscious are one, but in a normal awakened state the Conscious mind is obscured by all those beliefs and prejudices of the Belief System; it is not willing to accept suggestions that do not conform with these beliefs. That is why we use hypnosis, but then again it depends on how deep the subject can go into a trance so that a suggestion will reach the SubConscious mind.

You will learn beliefs called rules—how to behave when at home, in the street, in society. You will learn positive beliefs, such as, "You can do that," or "You will succeed in life." You will also learn limiting beliefs, such as, "You are a stupid boy," or "You are a failure." You will learn religious beliefs. Taken together, there are uncountable beliefs. All dos and don'ts are based on beliefs. There are different beliefs in different continents, in different religions, in different castes, in men and women, and so on.

Your parents did this to you because their parents did the same to them and they do not know better. On the other hand, you cannot imagine yourself living in a society without any beliefs; your beliefs are your membership card to your society. Beliefs can be very powerful; a limiting belief can ruin your life, in the same way a positive belief can be the reason for your success. Albert Einstein once said, "Common sense is the collection of prejudices acquired by the age of eighteen." In other words, common sense is a Belief System.

Religious beliefs in particular can do a lot of harm because they introduce fear in you, and **fear is the basis of all wrongdoing**. In the twentieth century alone more than 150 million people have been killed mostly because of religious beliefs. Every religion believes its god is the only true one, and most of them promise you a heaven if you behave according to their religious laws and a hell if you don't behave well. The truth is that there are no heavens and no hells. Right and wrong form part of most Belief System. In Universal Consciousness, right and wrong do not exist; right and wrong are judgments invented by our Belief System. There is nothing right or wrong in the universe. Everything is as it is, and things just are. Universal God is experiencing Itself, It experiences the greatest horrors and the most sublime emotions; it's all a play. Everybody is Universal God, and nobody is good or bad. It is our Belief System that make our acts good and bad. Each Consciousness behaves according to its spiritual evolution. There will come a day when we will see each other as one, when all beliefs will be superseded and eliminated. We will recognize our oneness with the universe; we will be illuminated, and we won't have to reincarnate anymore. We will dispose of our worldly identity, and we will be one with Universal Consciousness.

Advanced studies are going on in hypnosis. You can hypnotize someone and tell the individual that he or she cannot see the person standing in front of him or her. The individual will open his or her eyes and won't see that person. You can then hold an object behind the person, and the individual will tell you what the object is. The hypnotized individual is looking straight through the person. You may also tell someone under deep hypnosis that the person cannot hear anything except your voice; you can then fire a gun close to the person's ear, and he or she won't hear it. The same goes for all the other senses. That is the power of the Sub-Conscious mind. Under deep hypnosis you can change all the senses of a person. You can make an onion taste like an apple, you can make excrement smell like perfume, you can make the person become deaf, you can see well-dressed people for naked people, and you can feel no pain while you have an open wound. Who are you? Your soul? Your mind? There is no you; there is no I. "You" are Consciousness, "I" am Consciousness, we are the very same Consciousness; we are all One. We will come back to all this.

Now, you can also take an Islamic man and convince him that he will go to heaven, where seventy-two virgins are waiting for him to have sex with if he blows himself up, and he will do it. You can tell a Roman Catholic that the Host is the body and blood of Jesus Christ and he will believe you. But, you may argue, it is in the Bible, and the Bible is written by God. The truth is that no book in particular has been written by God, or, still better, all books are written by Universal Consciousness, including this one, because I am a part of Universal Consciousness, you are a part of the Universal Consciousness, and we are all Universal Consciousness. There is but one Universal Consciousness, and everything happens through It.

Placebos are another good example of Belief Systems. A physician may give a pill of sugar to a patient and tell the person it is a medicine and he or she will be cured. In experiments, sleeping pills have been given to people who were told the pill is to keep them awake the whole night, and they stayed awake. It can also happen the other way around. Thousands of examples can be given. It is all the same: whatever the person firmly believes in the Sub-Conscious mind will be accomplished.

But you may ask, what then is reality? If by reality you mean the material world you see around you, then actually there is no reality. You see, all reality is created by Consciousness and is interpreted by Consciousness. Because the reality is a material reality, therefore it is interpreted by Consciousness through the five senses of our body; if there were no Consciousness, there would be no material world, no so-called reality. We will elaborate on this in Chapter 4.

All beliefs are self-fulfilling prophecies. Sooner or later everything you firmly believe in will come true. You can accomplish whatever you want in this world. I repeat: whatever you want. Your thoughts supported by your faith will become creation. By faith I mean a firm knowledge that something is a fact. But someone could also stick to a false belief as if it were a fact; then this will also realize given the necessary time. We could give multiple examples of how the power of your Sub-Conscious mind will convert your beliefs into facts.

The reason for your caretakers to impose a Belief System upon you is that they didn't know any better; their parents did the same to them, and, as a matter of fact, you will be doing the same to your children. For parents to implant their beliefs into their children is usually considered a matter of responsibility in the raising of children. Besides, your parents would like you to behave according to their norms, and the best way to succeed in this is by imprinting you with their Belief System. It is to their comfort that you behave as they want you to, and they believe it is also to your convenience to behave as all other people do in the society you are going to form part of.

On the other hand, why did you peacefully accept such a load of beliefs from your parents, family members, teachers and priest? When you were very young you had no options. You were an infant without the mental capacity for reasoning in favor or against all these instructions. You were confined to a physical and mental dependency. When you got older, it was to your advantage, at least temporarily, to behave according to the impositions of your caretakers because in this way you could continue to count on their life-sustaining attention. Finally, as we said before, the Belief System they imposed on you became your "membership card" for the acceptance by the society you live in.

There are many more limiting beliefs that withhold you from having a much more ample understanding of the world you live in. You trust your government, your religion, and your social institutions. You trust them all so much that you do not bother to investigate all the corruption taking place in their organizations. There is corruption going on in the banks, there is corruption going on in governments, and there is corruption going on in religious institutions, especially in the Roman Catholic Church. But we just live on. We take delight in feasting, we amuse in squandering, we lavish in worldly pleasures. **It is now time that we invest some time in spiritual practices, in reading a good book, in listening to some classical music, in spending some more time in contact with nature, in just being with ourselves through contemplation and meditation.** Gerry Spence said, "I would rather have a mind opened by wonder than one closed by belief."

Due to improper lifestyle, 340 million people are suffering from depression in the world, 140 million people in the world have alcohol-related problems, fifty million people are regular drug users, and there are five million deaths each year related to smoking. There are 925 million people suffering from hunger and thirty-three million suffering from AIDS.

We live too much by what we have; if you are what you have, then who are you the day you do not have what you have now? Live by what you are! What you are stays with you while you evolve continuously in your beliefs! You are your spiritual values. You are the peace and love you can offer others! This is what this book is about. It hopes to offer you spiritual values, and it shows you how to live by universal values you are born with.

Let go of fear; fear springs from ignorance. Let go of ignorance. Study more, seek to know more instead of believing in stupidities such as "You are born in sin…" or "God will punish you…" or "There is a hell…" Let go of those limiting beliefs that stand in your way! Voltaire said, "Those who can make you believe absurdities can make you commit atrocities." It is absurd to believe that seventy-two virgins will be waiting for you in heaven if you commit the atrocity of blowing yourself up killing as many infidels as possible; that is one of the several beliefs of the Islamic religion. Also the dogmas of the Catholic Church are absurd leading to atrocities like the crusades and the inquisition. Many more examples can be mentioned.

It is those false beliefs that stand in your way and restrain you from realizing you are Consciousness. These beliefs obscure and hinder Consciousness from exhibiting its unlimited power. You are an intrinsic part of Universal Consciousness.

Change your life! The universe is abundant in joy and love, and you deserve all of it! Let nothing stand in your way! You spring from the Universal Consciousness! You are worthy! Go for it!

Chapter 3
EMOTIONS

Though emotions spring forth in connection with outside events, the emotion itself is always inside you and it is not directly produced by the outside event although the event may be the initial trigger to elicit the emotion. Further, whereas a series of processes takes place in your brain and the rest of your body with every emotion, it is nevertheless not true that emotions are generated by your brain although they may leave a trace in your neurological processes. Emotions are a choice made by conscious beings, and most of them are associated with the Belief System of the person who makes the choice. Let's take an example. Imagine a woman sitting in a train. A man sitting next to her, but unknown to her, suddenly puts his hand on her legs; let's call this an event. Since childhood she has learned from her parents that you should never allow a stranger to touch you, especially if he is a man; this is part of her Belief System. Based on this belief, she considers this man to be impertinent. The thought of impertinence toward her makes her feel offended and angry, and she chooses the emotions of offense and anger in light of her belief. She stands up abruptly and slaps him; this results to be her reaction when confronting this type of offense (another person might have chosen a different reaction). So, a simplified version of the sequence of what has been going on in her is this: Event ▶ Belief ▶ Thought ▶ Emotion ▶ Reaction. The reaction of the woman now becomes an event for the man, and a similar sequence starts all over, but this time in him. It is in this way that all of us interact with each other all the time. Your reaction is an event in my world, and my reaction is an event in your world.

In the preceding example, figure out for yourself what would have been the emotion and reaction chosen by the woman if the man sitting next to her would have been her beloved husband instead of a stranger. Being happily together at that moment, things would have turned out very different; what does this reveal? It tells us that it is *not the event itself* that triggers the emotion but the evaluation based on a belief connected to that particular event. What is an event if it is not evaluated? It is "that." And what is "that"? It is "that"—it is nothing, it has no value whatsoever. There is nothing in the universe that has an intrinsic value, that is, nothing has a value by and of itself. Values are assigned by Conscious beings, and for this to occur it is necessary that the Conscious being considers his- or herself as separated from the object, the person, or the event in the outside world. As you will see in later chapters, this separation is a paradox because actually all that exists is Consciousness and because Consciousness is omnipresent, separation in a real sense cannot exist. Objects and events in the world have no value by and of themselves; they are assigned a value when they are interpreted by a Conscious being and the interpretation is based on beliefs. You can thus understand that two people and also two populations with unlike beliefs will interpret and value differently a same event, and consequently their emotional response will be different.

So, every time something happens to you, you are dominated by an emotion that you will consider as inevitable and natural; but this, however, is not so. Actually, your Belief System functions as a filter. When you have to choose a belief, you choose out of thousands the one you think will offer you most pleasure, the one you think is more convenient at that particular moment, and so **you generate your own emotions**, you create your own world. Also remember that most of the beliefs that control your life, that is, the beliefs that have you living on "automatic pilot," are in your subconscious mind; you are not constantly aware of them.

If you are continually troubled by unpleasant emotions and your life is ruled more by burden than by peace, it is time to bring about a change in your Belief System. Remember, you evaluate the world and you choose your emotions according to your beliefs. You cannot change the world but you can change your beliefs, and **as soon as you change a particular belief, your interpretation of the world** *based on that belief* **will change.** Giving due consideration to the following concepts may help you bring about a change in your belief system and may pave the way for a more flexible way of living:

- *In essence* we are all the same and we are all one. Our essential being is Consciousness, and there is but one Consciousness in the universe. So, everything you do in favor or against another person you are actually doing to yourself and vice versa.
- Everything a person does is done in search of pleasure, of well-being; the contrary is pain. We

differ from each other in what we derive pleasure from, and in our way of seeking it.
- Always keep in mind that all is perishable; life is an ongoing process of transformation and evolution; nothing "out there" lasts forever.
- Live in the present; the past is a present that is already gone and the future is a present still to come. Properly speaking, past and future do not exist; all that exists is NOW. We believe in past and future because we believe in the transition of linear time. The constant swaying between past and future is a definite source of suffering; it creates instability and fear. **The only moment you truly live is NOW.**

Emotions and Belief System

Emotions happen because you interpret and evaluate an event with your Belief System. So, consider this: 1) If you do not interpret and evaluate an event, no emotion whatsoever will arise in you. 2) Because the interpretation and evaluation depend on your Belief System, emotions will vary with each person, with each nationality, with each culture, with circumstances, and so on. 3) You can have control over your emotions by changing your Belief System. 4) Emotions should not be confused with feelings such as hunger and thirst, which are biological reactions.

Love

Love is a force. It is the force of attraction. When you love someone, you seek to be close to her or him as with your parents, your children, and many others. As we will show later, love can be considered a force rather than an emotion; it is the force of attraction. The main component of love is freedom; **true and pure love is**

unconditional. True love is to accept somebody the way he or she is without trying to change him or her to your demands. Very few human beings are capable of loving like this, but through the teachings in this book and other books, and with some training, you will be able to do this. Keep in mind that *the ultimate goal of spiritual growth is to reach true and pure unconditional love.*

Fear is the absence of love and may be considered as a force of separation.

Emotions the Brain and the Mind

Your brain contains 1.1 trillion cells, of which one hundred billion are neurons. The neurons are the cells that receive and send messages from and to your whole body; every second there may be quadrillions of electromagnetic signals going through your brain. It is my opinion that all these signals are recorded in the ethereal body of your soul and form your true memory. When you leave this world, you as Consciousness enveloped by your soul take all these memories with you and based on these memories you will, together with your spiritual guide and masters, decide where your next incarnation will be, who are going to be your parents, and what will be the main experiences you will be going through. There are scientists who believe that emotions are stored in your brain because when, during an operation, they touch specific parts of your brain certain emotions or events will be elicited. If our memories were stored in our brain then they would all be gone when we died. If you believe in reincarnation, then memory of all previous lives must be conserved. There are methods to go to previous lives and also to your spiritual life just before this incarnation.

It is part of the Belief System of almost everybody that God is the only being that offers unconditional love. On the other hand, those same people who believe that God's love is unconditional also believe that God puts demands on them and that when they do not comply with his demands He will punish them. There is a contradiction in beliefs here: either God's love is unconditional and he does not punish us, or his love is not unconditional and he might punish us. The point is this: you should not abstain from wrongdoing out of fear for being punished by any judge or by God. You should abstain from wrongdoing out of responsibility and respect for your kindred; if I love you, I won't inflict any harm whatsoever on you. All wrongdoings are fundamentally an act of fear and thus a lack of love; the purpose of life is to grow spiritually and become one with your essence, which is Universal Pure Love, that is, Universal Consciousness-God.

All human beings are in need of love from the date of their conception and birth to the date of their death. There are, however, certain ages when it is of crucial priority for a human being to receive signs of love. From birth to around the age of seven, it is of utmost importance for children to receive continual signs of love from their parents or caretakers in the form of caresses and embraces, as this will stimulate the growth of neurons and synapses in the brain of the newborn and play a major role in the child's psychological and intellectual development. From seven to fourteen (don't take the ages too precisely), children still need the love fully, but by now they are also permeated by the feeling of security, although they might not yet know the meaning of the word *security* itself. For them the feeling of security goes with, "I am surrounded by a house," "I have a bed to sleep on," "I have clothing to wear," "I have food to eat," and *most important of all*, "I can always rely on the affectionate support of two very knowledgeable persons called Mom and Dad." Children think their parents know a lot because they are constantly telling them what to do and what not to do; for more on this, go back to the formation of your Belief System in chapter 2.

Then something unforeseen may happen during this period of love and security. Mom and Dad get involved in constant quarrels, the peace at home is disturbed by their threatening yells, and slapping takes place. The (say) eight-year-old child faces all this with bewilderment. The boy or girl cannot understand why two loving people of such good judgment are inflicting pain to each other. The child feels powerless, does not know how to mediate, and his or her world of love and security starts disintegrating. Then comes the most devastating blow: Dad abandons home. The child wonders why Dad did not ask for his or her opinion before leaving, and the child's not yet mature mind may come up with this answer: "Because I am not good enough. Because, after all, he does not love me that much." The child feels desolated. One of his or her pillars of security has failed, and the love and trust he or she relied on have waned. It is very probable that during adolescence and adulthood, the child will be afflicted by inferiority complex and lack of self-esteem. As a matter of fact, most of the bullies walking around are people who did not receive the corresponding love during their childhood; deep within, the bully is tormented by fear while at the same time in desperate need of love.

The previous two paragraphs are a call to parents to pay due attention to the rearing of their children. You don't show love to children by just giving them toys to play with and putting some food on the table; true love is given by affectionate hugging and caressing. Nowadays an alarming number of children are subjugated to violent computer games and lousy TV programs. When, besides these detrimental games and programs, children do not receive affection from their parents, then the feeling of kindness and love will become as an alien to them, and this may result in mental disabilities in their adult life.

Fear

Fear is an emotion that produces separation and destruction. Look again at the two examples we gave in the first paragraph. When you are angry, you fear the disturbance being applied to your comfort zone and you may either run away from the person causing you the pain or you may attack the individual. When you are jealous, you fear losing your loved one and you may cause harm to the ones causing you the pain.

Fear is the most negative emotion there can be, and it will always have pathological consequences. Take the following example: You do something ▶ you consider that what you did is wrong ▶ you feel guilty and because you feel guilty you consider that you deserve to be punished ▶ punishment is pain and you don't want more pain ▶ you feel fear ▶ not being able to do anything about the whole situation, you get desperate and angry ▶ under the pressure of desperation and anger, you do something that most likely will be considered again as wrongdoing; you have now closed the circle, and the sequence will be repeated. The distortion in this sequence of events and feelings is in your belief that you did "something wrong." This belief makes you "feel guilty," and this feeling will stir in you the belief that "you deserve to be punished." Here again you can see how beliefs and emotions are intertwined and that your state of happiness is directly connected to your Belief System.

Here you can see again the control that beliefs have in your life. If you have beliefs that continually make you choose emotions of pain, get rid of them. Don't stay with beliefs that produce more pain than pleasure. Don't be afraid of growing spiritually. Let go of beliefs that make you choose pain emotions. Transform them! Do it now!

When you understand how the universe works, as I will explain later, you will also understand that **there is no wrongdoing** in the sense of sin against a God. At every moment in your life, you do the best you are capable of doing at that particular moment—that is, you do whatever it is you feel like doing to supply you with more peace and pleasure or with less stress and pain. Always keep in mind that Consciousness-God does not punish anybody nor does He reward anybody. Because you believe in wrongdoing, therefore you believe in punishment, and you abstain from wrongdoing out of fear for punishment. Actually, you "punish" yourself because the belief in wrongdoing generates the feeling of guilt, which is an unpleasant feeling and which may be considered as "punishment" for your "wrongdoing." As to reward, when you favor someone you feel pleasurable when you see the person happy, and that feeling of pleasure may be considered as your reward.

There are religions that demand from their followers to fear God and at the same time to love God. How could you love somebody and at the very same time fear him? When you love somebody, you seek his company. When you fear somebody, you run away from him; you cannot do both at *the same time* and with *the same person* in mind. Further, if you constantly live with fear for somebody, your love for him will ultimately wane.

There is something ironic about fear: the more you run away from it, the more you attract it. Why is this? Because if you intensely fear something, you are most probably thinking frequently about it, and it's no wonder the fear may realize. Fear is absence of love. When we fear we run away from the feared person or circumstance, and when we love we seek closeness. As I said before, you cannot feel fear and love at the same time for the same person. Trying to do this creates confusion and anxiety.

Fear plays a fundamental role in most psychological problems. Of course, fear can also trigger a convenient reaction. In the presence of a serious peril you will react with the "fight or flight" response, that is, if you think you can control the danger you will fight, and if not, you will flight; both responses are survival reactions.

Most of the time, when fear is related to psychological or religious beliefs, *you increase the fear by running away from it.* How does that work? Well, what you are afraid of is a belief—*it is a condition inside yourself.* By constantly thinking of how you can get rid of the motive of your fear, you transform it, as if it were in an object "out there." You keep running, fighting, avoiding, and the fear just gains in strength. The point is that the way you try to get rid of the fear is just what aggravates the fear; the object of fear is not "out there," it is "in here." It is caused by a belief, and you cannot run away from a belief; the belief is an intimate part of yourself. Nonetheless, you can learn to have control over your fears and live a happier life. In the following paragraphs I will lead you through the necessary steps to accomplish this.

Control over Your Emotions

Let us start with your emotions. Your emotions that seemed to be originated by an event or by someone "out there" are actually generated deep within you. Your emotions are chosen, and the choice depends on your interpretation of what happened "out there," and the interpretation has its foundation on your Belief System. So, how can you control your emotions? You can do this by living much more consciously of how your emotions of pain intrude into your life. Let us take an example. In the example I will substitute the letters "xyz" for any obscene word. Now, you have learned from childhood that to be called "xyz" is a serious offense. It is a matter of honor, of dignity, of respect, and you should never let anybody call you "xyz." This belief about the value of "xyz" will make you choose without further consideration the emotion of offense when you hear this word. But, "xyz" **has no intrinsic value**. It is assigned a value by your Belief System. **The moment you change your belief about the meaning of "xyz," you will stop choosing offense as response to the word "xyz."** Ask yourself the following questions: Where did the offense come from? Did the offense come out of the mouth of the person who pronounced the word "xyz"? No, the offense is in your interpretation of the meaning, value, or scope of "xyz" based on your Belief System. Consider this: What is "xyz"? Actually "xyz" is a sound, but this sound has been assigned a particular meaning in a system called language. It is now called an obscene word. Now, this word is like thousands of other words, but you have been programmed in your Belief System to feel offended when you hear this particular word, so, according to your Belief System, you now choose the emotion of offense. **But the offense is not in the word.**

It is in the meaning and the value that you attach to the word in your Belief System; *it is your decision to feel offended.*

Now suppose you take the decision to seriously start practicing control over your emotions by not attaching a painful value to the word "xyz," but then suddenly a new fear pops up under the disguise of the feelings called *pride and shame.* You are here again at the starting point: Belief System; pride and shame are based on the fear of what others would think about you in specific circumstances. You do not dare to lose face in the presence of family members and friends by not showing anger when you "have been offended." But why care what others think about you if you hold a high self-esteem of yourself? Actually it is so that **the less esteem you have for yourself the more you care about what others think about you.** Now you are in a trap! If you do not have a high esteem of yourself you are in pain, and if others do not give you the esteem you so much desire then again you are in pain. And why do you desire esteem from others? *Because you do not have esteem for yourself!* You desire the esteem that is missing in you! **Stop desiring esteem from others; you are God-Consciousness. You have all the esteem of the Universe. GO FOR IT!**

To be at peace with yourself, you must know that there are no degrees of better or worse in the universe. Everything in the universe is indispensable and everything is as it should be at any particular moment. Forget pride and shame! Always remember this: you are unique and you are as you should be at this moment, and again at the next moment, and so ad infinitum. Life is change, continuous change, but with every change you are again as you should be after that change. **So, forget to choose offense when you hear "xyz" and choose to**

be happy! And forget about the destructive and limiting emotions of pride and shame; choose to be happy, to be happy NOW!

Further Steps toward Change

Your Belief System is so deep rooted and firmly fixed in you that continually you are inclined to confuse your beliefs with reality, with indisputable facts. As I will show in later chapters, there is no reality "out there." Your reality is "in here," in your conscious interpretation of the world. Let me take again the example of the obscene sound "xyz." This sound is a word within *your language system and your Belief System* to which you react with the emotion of offense because you have been taught to do so. You have also learned that if you do not feel offended you are a coward, you have no concept of honor, of principles, of dignity, and so on. But, you can also look at it in a totally different way. The word "xyz" is just a sound, a word-sound like thousands of others. Become aware that you have heard this word-sound but *do not attach an emotional value to it.* It is just a word-sound pronounced by an angry person. As long as you do not attach any value to it, it won't inflict you any distress. You may feel compassion for the resentful person who pronounced it, but just leave it there. Nobody can harm you if you don't allow that person to. It is written that a wise man called Jesus once said, "If they slap you on one cheek, offer them the other cheek." What did this wise man mean by this? It may well be that he meant, *"I am beyond your offense.* You may try again and again, but I won't let your actions hurt me." You too can do this. You can practice to grow beyond offense.

The bottom line is this: interpret whatever you derive from your senses, become aware of what it is, but do not attach an emotional value to it that will cause you pain.

A word is a word, it is a sound, it does *not intrinsically* have a value that can cause you pain; it is for you to decide whether you want to attach pain to it. Let me repeat this once more: the word by and of itself is not the offense. *You generate the feeling of offense* by the value you attach to the word, and the value is in your Belief System; the same is true for any event.

If we could all accept that we are actually one in Consciousness, that to inflict harm on others is to inflict harm on ourselves and vice versa, that if we could be more compassionate instead of fearing and distrusting each other, that if we could see equality in everyone instead of discriminating each other by race, caste, nationality, religion, and power positions, that if a majority of us could do all that, we would certainly be living in a world with less rejection, hate, conflicts, and wars and certainly with less fear because, ultimately, it is fear that is at the root of all circumstances we blame for our suffering.

Why Do We Refrain From Change?

Everybody fears the *unknown*. As a general rule, the *unknown* produces *pain,* while the *known* produces *pleasure.* The basic reason we refrain from change is because in change we confront an unknown situation. ***Successful people are those who accept the unknown as a challenge.***

There are people who are so attached to their personality that they refrain from change; they do not want a known "me" to disappear and a new, unknown "me" to appear. It is as if the first "me" dies, and nobody wants to die. But, on the other hand, a new "me" is born, a spiritually more advanced "me"; that is what life is about: change, transformation, less fear, more love. The greatest unknown is death, so almost everyone is afraid of dying, but there is no death. There is only getting born again, and again, continuous change. Whether you want it or not, you have to accept change; some change very slowly, some go much faster, but everyone has to change. Everyone is getting born again and again. **You must consciously "die" while you are alive so that you can be consciously alive while you are "dying";** think about this.

Forgiveness

Much of the pain most people carry with them is engraved in the feeling of resentment from past events. Every time you think of what he or she did to you, you feel anger, you become bitter. There is only one remedy against this, and that is forgiveness. There are people who say, "I can forgive but I cannot forget." The point is that, properly speaking, forgiving and forgetting have nothing to do one with the other. You cannot forget an event because it is engraved in your soul, but that does not prevent you from forgiving. How do you know when you have forgiven a person? You have forgiven a person when you no longer feel resentment when thinking back about the "offensive event" the individual inflicted on you; you may feel pity or at the most indifference but not bitterness and anger. On the other hand, you have not forgiven a person when every time you think back about what he or she did to you, you are bothered by resentment and anger.

One way to deal with forgiveness is to think of every person as the sum of his or her resources. Resources are the actions you are capable of taking in any particular moment; your resources may be physical or mental. You can only do, and you actually only do, what your resources permit you to do at a particular moment. You always choose the resource that supplies you with the most of pleasure, the one you feel the most comfortable with. Consider the following example. Suppose you take a five-dollar bill out of your pocket to pay for something and at that very moment a beggar boy, who happens to be nearby, grabs the bill out of your hand, runs away with it, and disappears among the crowd. The first feeling you choose is of helplessness and some anger. Later that day you sit at home, and while sipping a cup of coffee you think about what happened, that is, you have the resource of reconsidering the whole event. You can ask yourself, what were the resources of this beggar boy? Can he earn his money by getting himself a decent job? The answer happens to be no. He has no education, he cannot pay for an education, and he has tried to get a job but did not succeed. Can he sit somewhere and beg for money? The answer may be yes, he can. He has done it many times, but people ignore him and sometimes even scold him, and at the end he never gets enough for a decent meal. Earlier that day he was very hungry, and in a moment of despair he decided to grab your money. *He did what his resources permitted him to do at that particular moment.* He is now finally enjoying a healthy meal. You feel **compassion**. Compassion is understanding for the feeling of the other and for yourself; you understand why he needed to rob you, and you also understand why you felt angry. You may now be more at peace with yourself. When you think back of the event you feel serene, ***you have forgiven.*** You feel released and you drink your coffee with a smile on your face.

Who are you? Are you your emotions? Are you your Belief System? The answer to the last two questions is no. You are beyond your emotions and your beliefs. You are Consciousness. You are a spark of the all-pervading Universal Consciousness. You are the force of pure love.

So, once more, if you are not happy about the way your life is going, then do something about it. Do not just sit there complaining and waiting for some sort of miracle to happen; miracles do not exist. Miracles are natural events of which we (still) do not understand the underlying cause. Miracles do not happen out of nothing. You produce "miracles" by taking the right and necessary actions. So, start today! Take action for the betterment of your life. Study more, meditate more, substitute empowering beliefs for limiting beliefs, see equality in everybody, accept yourself, and accept others. Go for intention. Conquer fear and engage in love. **Go for it!**

Almost all people blame the world for their suffering. For every offense there is a culprit, for all their sufferings there is some event in the world to be blamed, and they insist on not taking any responsibility for their emotions; it is always the "others" who are the bad guys and the cause of their unhappiness. Let us realize that if a great number of us take the necessary steps to change, we would be living in a better world, a world without so much offense, without so much blame, with less resentment and conflicts. We are all a spark of the all-pervading Universal Consciousness, we are ONE, and there is no separation. Because we are enclosed in a material body, we seem to distinguish a "you" and a "me," but spiritually we are ONE. So put your arms on the shoulders of the person in front of you while you look in his or her eyes and say, "I am you. You are me. We are ONE." Then he or she will put his arms on your shoulders and say, "You are me. I am you. We are ONE." Then you will embrace each other. I suggest this to be the way we greet each other from now on.

You may say I'm a dreamer. Yes, I am, but there are dreams that come true. Marcel Proust once said, "If a little dream is dangerous, the cure for it is not to dream less, but to dream more, to dream all the time."

Universal Consciousness, Emotions, and Creation
In animals, plants, and minerals, emotions or emotion-like reactions take place through instincts, learned behaviors, or reflexes. In human beings they are predominantly a reaction to belief-evaluation systems. It is my opinion that there are no emotions in the pure Consciousness world. Universal-God-Consciousness does not feel emotions. We thus might explain the reason for the incarnation of Consciousness in the material world. I believe that Consciousness-God incarnates in the material world in order to undergo all emotions and occurrences, and thus experience Its Self.

There is only one Being in the universe, and that is Consciousness. If you insist that there must be a god, then you can call this being Consciousness-God. Now, Consciousness is indispensable for the creation of the universe; Consciousness creates and maintains the universe. There is only Consciousness. You as an entity do not exist. I as an entity do not exist. Only Consciousness exists and we are all, and everything is, a creation of Consciousness.

Emotions do not exist by themselves. They are elicited in our thoughts by evaluating events through our Belief System. They are a resource to feel pleasure, or pain, or indifference, and Consciousness experiences the world through them. Train yourself to choose healthy emotions, for instance, by listening to a relaxing piece of music, to enjoy a landscape, to be with your family in peace and love.

Chapter 4
WHAT IS REALITY

Now that you know that the evaluation of your world depends on your Belief System and that also your emotions are influenced by the same system, it is proper for you to wonder whether there is anything whatsoever "out there" that has a totally independent existence. Well, amazing as it may sound, the answer is no, there is nothing whatsoever that is not affected by Consciousness because everything is (a degree of) Consciousness; Consciousness is the only reality there is. All that happens in the universe is Consciousness becoming aware of Itself in its infinite manifestations in the mineral, plant, animal, and human world.

But, you may insist, like most people, that there must be a tangible, solid, and indisputable reality out there that is not transformed in any way when you perceive it through your five senses; you may think that this world is perceived exactly as it is through your senses of sight, hearing, touch, smell, and taste. That this reality is tangible I may agree with you, although it is not necessarily solid. As you know, matter is built up of molecules, and these in turn are composed of atoms. Simplistically speaking, an atom consists of a nucleus in which the protons and neutrons are packed together, and of electrons encircling the nucleus at very high velocities. Let us take as an example the atom of hydrogen consisting of only one proton and one electron; its diameter is ten millionth of a millimeter and the proton in the center is one hundred thousand times smaller than the diameter. This will render that more than 99.9999999 percent of the atom is empty space and thus not solid. The reason objects appear as solid is that the electrons encircle the nucleus of the atom at a velocity of approximately two thousand kilometers per second, which means that every second they will go around the nucleus approximately seven billion times; this makes you feel as if you are touching solid material. Another reason is that the negative charge of the electrons of a solid object repels the negative charge of the electrons on your body, and the object results as impenetrable.

Reality is a whole, reality is the whole of the infinite universe, the only reality is Consciousness. When you try to study a part of reality, that part becomes the object and you are the subject. But now various anomalies take place. First, reality is an undivided whole, and as soon as you sever a part of the whole you actually miss the absolute picture. Second, you, the subject, are yourself part of the object that is reality; every study of reality is a study of yourself. If you try to detach a part of reality in order to study it, it happens that what is being studied is what is doing the study; what you try to look at is the one that is looking; it is absolute knowledge trying to acquire part of knowledge. The only way of understanding reality is by becoming reality. Third, to describe reality you use "language," but language is itself an illusion, it is a metaphor; that is why the Taoists say, "Those who know do not speak; those who speak do not know." On the other hand, to describe something, we have no other option but to use language.

Reality is infinite, Consciousness-God is infinite, and everything is Consciousness-God. If you separate God from the rest of the universe, you make It finite, and then the rest of the universe is outside Its control. All supposed finites are reflections in the mirror of infinite; let us call this infinite: Consciousness-God or, for short, God. We are reflections in the mirror of the infinite God. If we set God (infinite) apart from us (supposedly finite), then God himself also becomes finite, and this cannot be. What we call God or Consciousness-God will always be infinite.

Reality as Perceived by Sight

But, how real is an object that we perceive through our senses? The answer is the object itself is not absolutely real. What is in a sense real is the image of the object that, through your mind, is interpreted by Consciousness. The image then attains the attribute of real *because* it is interpreted by Consciousness. If there were no Consciousness there would be no image, no reality either "outside" or "inside," nothing would exist. ***Consciousness is the prime and sole existence***; the so-called material world is a form adapted by Consciousness for its own convenience.

Further, when you look at an object, you take it for granted that you are perceiving precisely the object you are looking at, but this, however, is not so. Let me explain. Sight is our ability to transform light "in here" into something apparently real that appears to be "out there." I will use the terms "in here" and "out there" as if there is an observer and an observed separated in space; this duality of observer/observed is not exactly so, but for the scope and extent of this book we will have to suffice with this illusion. Now, the presence of light is an indispensable condition for human beings to experience what we call sensuous seeing; in the absence of light sensuous seeing is not possible. Light forms a narrow part of the broad spectrum of electromagnetic energy. With our normal sight, human beings can see wavelengths only between 380 and 740 nanometers of the electromagnetic spectrum. When light impinges on a subject, say a red car, most of the light's wavelengths are absorbed by the material of the car and only wavelengths around 680 nanometers are reflected and reach our eyes, traveling at a speed of approximately 300,000 kilometers per second. In the back of our eyes are about eighteen million light-sensing cells called cones and rods. These cells transform the reflected wavelengths of light into an electrochemical signal that travels through our optic nerves to the brain. When this signal reaches a certain part in the back of our brain, Consciousness, via the life force, or soul, interprets this signal and becomes aware of "seeing a red car."

So, a stimulus from a particular wavelength of light, via photosensitive cells in the eyes, is transformed in an electrochemical signal and what you believe to be seeing "out there" as something you have learned to call "car" with a color you have learned to call "red" is not "out there," it is "in here." You do not see "out there," you see "in here"; if there were no conscious being around, nothing would be seen. There would be no phenomenon of sight. When the corresponding electrochemical signals reach a certain area of the occipital lobe of the brain, then Consciousness via your soul perceives an **image** called **car** of a **color** called **red**. There is no red on the car, there is no color red traveling from the car to your brain; it is light with a wavelength of 680 nanometers that travels. **Light per se, no matter of what wavelength, has no color**; the quality of red is a learned creation of Consciousness. If the reflected wavelength had been 460 nanometers, you would have said that you are seeing a color you have learned to call blue. The names of the colors (Belief System) have been taught to you by your parents; all colors are just names in the metaphor of language. Colors are wavelengths expressed in words; I can never be absolutely sure that I see "red" (or any other color) in exactly the same way that you see it. You cannot know what the object "out there" is like precisely. You only get to know an image of the object. We could still go another step further: what is "out there" is also Consciousness; matter and life force, or soul, or mind, are a state of Consciousness. Matter-Mind-Consciousness—by analogy ice, liquid, and steam are different states of water. (Sometimes I use "mind" instead of the word "soul.") Finally, and this is very important, your Belief System has an influence on what and how you see the world, and thus we can say that you don't see things as they are, you see things as you are.

On the other hand, please note that if your eyes, your optical nerve, or your brain have some sort of shortcoming, then your mind cannot transmit to Consciousness the same image as that of someone who does not have any anomaly. There is a stringent relationship between your Consciousness-mind and your body, particularly with your brain; anything that happens in your Consciousness-mind reverberates in your brain-body, and anything that happens in your brain-body has an effect on your Consciousness-mind. To make this better understandable, let us use an analogy. Say a TV station sends out a program. If your TV receiver has a defect, you will receive a distorted image on your TV screen. Compare the signal from the TV station to a stimulus being conveyed to you from "out there." Now compare the TV set to your brain, and finally, compare the "you" viewing the program to your Consciousness-mind. Of course you cannot interpret the distorted incoming signal clearly, although the broadcast signal is flawless. So, if someone has a disorder somewhere in his or her nervous system, the mind and Consciousness will receive and interpret a distorted image, and this distorted image becomes the "reality" of this particular person.

Tribes of Eskimos, of Bushmen, and of certain Indians in the Amazon have a different concept of color from people living in a city. There are certain shades of colors they distinguish better than us, and there are other colors we see and that they don't see or see only vaguely. This also has something to do with language. We create certain words to denote certain experiences. It is an intricate study to determine exactly when an interpretation has to do more with language, with the color, or with brain function. Consciousness creates a word to denote an experience that is repeatedly presented through the brain. If the experience is not repeated and if it has no survival value, then Consciousness may not label it with a word. This leads us to another aspect of reality, and that is that language is just a metaphor. Language is just a symbolic representation of an object, but it is not the object.

The very first thing created by Consciousness is light. It shines the light through the field of energy that permeates the universe. Then, by the will of intention, It desires to create something, anything, and it appears in the world similar to a hologram; **all creation is light**.

Reality as Perceived by Hearing

When it concerns hearing, the following will take place. Suppose a person "A" says hello to you. A rush of air flows out of the lungs of person A. The air strikes the person's vocal cords and makes them vibrate. By the time this vibration leaves the person's mouth, it will have a frequency between twenty and twenty thousand hertz (cycles per second), and it will travel at a velocity of approximately 340 meters per second. This vibration reaches your ear canal and will cause your eardrum to vibrate. The vibration is then transferred to three tiny bones, and from these it travels to another bone structure called the cochlea. The cochlea is filled with a fluid and special nerve cells that convert the vibration into electrochemical nerve impulses. Via the auditory nerve these impulses travel through the brain to two zones known as the Wernicke and Brocca zones, and here these impulses are interpreted as sound, specifically as "hello." Now, we can ask, who or what interprets the brain impulses as "hello," who or what transforms the brain impulses in the word-sound "hello"? Is it done by the brain? The answer is a straight no. The interpretation is done by Consciousness, by you-Consciousness. There was *no sound* coming out of the mouth of person A, there was *no sound* between the person's mouth and your ears, there was *no sound* between your ears and your brain; there was only a plain wave with a frequency between twenty and twenty thousand hertz up to the moment it was transformed in an electrochemical signal and interpreted by Consciousness. Only then did it become **sound** and specifically "hello." So, sound has no intrinsic existence; certain ranges of frequencies become "sound" **when they are interpreted by Consciousness.**

The Reality of Touch, Smell, and Taste.

Whatever we perceive through touch, smell, or taste is also a matter of interpretation by Consciousness. The stimulus received through touch is a difference in pressure or temperature on our skin. Consciousness interprets the differences as pleasurable or painful or as heat or cold. In smell and taste, specific molecules are responsible for the stimulus, but the particular tastes and smells are not properties of the molecules themselves; again, the interpretation lies in Consciousness via the mind, via certain areas of the brain. So, allow me to insist that there are certain molecules and ions emanating from the surface of fruits, flowers, food, and other substances. These molecules per se don't carry a particular taste or odor, but they do have the property of stimulating the taste or olfactory system, and the stimulus is interpreted by Consciousness, via the brain and the mind, as a particular taste or smell.

Is There No Reality at All "Out There"?

There may be something "out there," but that something is composed of Consciousness and it can be interpreted only by Consciouness. But, are there any material objects in the universe at locations where there is *no Consciousness?* Wrong question, because **Universal Consciousness is all pervading; in every billionth of a millimeter of space there is Consciousness**. Where there is material, there is Consciousness because Consciousness creates material. Material itself is a degree of Consciousness. **Consciousness is all that exists.**

Entanglement and Nonlocality

In quantum mechanics it has been shown that once two particles have been in contact with each other, that is, once they are correlated or entangled, they will always have an influence on each other whatever the distance. Take electrons "A" and "B," which have been part of the same atom. Once they are separated, no matter by what distance, if the spin of particle A is altered, particle B will alter its spin correspondingly. The same goes for Consciousness. All "individual" consciousnesses derive from Universal Consciousness. Now, anything, and I mean **anything**, that happens to you **will be known and have an effect on the whole universe.** This applies to every single individual, and from this we derive Parallel Universes. Every single thought, emotion, action, and decision that is taken by you and by **everyone else in the whole universe** has an influence on **everyone else in the whole universe**. We are all instantaneously connected with each other. Once again: **WE ARE ALL ONE.**

The Holographic Universe

Another interesting aspect of the wholeness of the universe is the hologram. A hologram is the image of an object that is obtained with a laser light setup. The resulting impression on a film can be projected in the space right in front of you. No screen is necessary. What's more: the image is three dimensional, meaning you can walk around it and view it from all sides. When you intend to touch it, your hand will go straight through it. Another property of the hologram is that when you cut the holographic film in two or more parts, each part will project the whole image. Now there is evidence that the universe works as a hologram, that is, that in each part of the universe the whole is included. Each cell of your body is a hologram of your whole body, and your body is a hologram of the whole universe. **We are all one in an infinite hologram.**

Particle and Wave—The Uncertainty Principle

The world appears to us as matter or as energy. Matter is built up of particles; energy is detected in the form of waves. There is an experiment in quantum mechanics called: The double-slit experiment. In this experiment you can detect whether a subatomic particle will behave as a particle or as a wave. Simply said, if you look at an electron in the experiment it will appear as a particle, and if you don't look it will appear as a wave. This is so because the mere fact of observing the electron changes its behavior; this applies to everything: Observing is modifying. What is the electron, a particle or a wave? It is both! So, it seems we will never know the absolute truth.

Werner Heisenberg, in his Principle of Uncertainty, states that we will never know the whole truth at the same time; you cannot, for example, determine the exact velocity and the exact position of an electron at the same time.

I accept all this to mean that there is no truth to be detected in the material world. All truth and all knowledge is in Consciousness. **The truth will be found the day Consciousness discovers Itself; you will be enlightened the day Consciousness becomes Self-Conscious. You cannot know the truth because you and the truth are one. You will know the truth when you consciously become the truth.**

The Only Reality Is Consciousness

Our senses are expressed by Consciousness interpreting the activities produced in the brain via the mind. Our emotions are expressed by Consciousness choosing a belief that would allow the emotion to arise. Our thoughts are generated by Consciousness wanting to disclose them. Finally, all reality has to do with Consciousness. Consciousness is the only reality; God is Consciousness and Consciousness is God. **God-Consciousness is all that exists.**

You don't exist and I do not exist; nothing material exists; only Consciousness exists.

The whole universe is filled by a field. This field is everywhere, and when I say everywhere I mean everywhere—inside and outside you, from an atom to the stars, just everywhere. This field, acknowledged by scientists, is known by different names, such as Zero-Point Energy Field, Cosmic Consciousness Field, Akashic Field or A-Field. I believe this field to be pure Consciousness, absolute Consciousness. Now, the absolute, all-pervading Consciousness cannot experience itself because it is absolute, it is sole, and it is omnipresent. Now, to experience itself, Consciousness "encloses" itself in material beings in the mineral, plant, and animal world, in atomic and subatomic particles, and in human beings, and so **It participates in every single experience through the material world.** It is thus that this becomes a participatory universe. Nothing is on itself. Everything is interconnected and everything participates in the creation of everything.

Consciousness, while enclosed in the container of your body, creates your world according to your Belief System; and this is the same for everybody. You create your world, I create my world. **Let us create a world of health, of peace and love, of abundance, and all this with every single being in mind. Let us forget "I," let us forget "you," let us forget "ego," let us forget "self." None of that exists. There is only one. Duality does not exist. Only Consciousness exists.**

Chapter 5
CONSCIOUSNESS

As we can deduce from the previous chapter, Consciousness is a sine qua non condition for experience to take place. How could you be reading this book if you were not conscious? How could I have written it if I were not conscious? But notice that these questions call for several other questions. Who or what are the "you" and the "I" who are conscious? Where is this consciousness located? Does Consciousness survive the demise of the body? What exactly is consciousness?

When studying something, there is an object and a subject; the object is what is being studied, and the subject is the one realizing the study. It so happens that in the case of Consciousness, the subject and the object are the same. It is for this reason that studying Consciousness is an almost impossible task; you can grasp the full understanding of Consciousness only when you *become* Consciousness, and when you *become* Consciousness, that is, when you are one with Consciousness, then you are enlightened. But then again, who is the "you" that becomes one with Consciousness? There is no "you" and there is no "I." There is only Consciousness! Let us have a closer look at all this.

There are two main branches in science when it concerns consciousness. One declares that consciousness is the direct result of brain processes and that it ceases to exist after the body dies. The other affirms that consciousness is not rigorously dependent on bodily processes and that it survives the demise of the body. Let us have a brief look at these two streams.

The first group consists of scientists who argue that consciousness is an epiphenomenon of the brain. This means that consciousness springs out of the brain processes. This would imply that consciousness is a stage in the evolutionary process of the brain. But, this being so, how can we explain that consciousness exhibits properties that far exceed any capacity of the body out of which it would have evolved? And further, which part of the brain specifically did consciousness outgrow? Innumerable physiological actions take place in our body in order to maintain the coherence of the whole. All these bodily actions are for the purpose of survival, but who or what makes the decisions to wake up late in the morning, to choose to have breakfast consisting of two scrambled eggs instead of a cheese sandwich, to decide to visit the Metropolitan Museum out of five others, to call one friend out of ten others and ask that person to join you for dinner at one particular restaurant out of twenty others, to choose to go to one particular movie out of twelve, to accept that your friend would pay for the entrance, to like or dislike the movie you just saw, to walk home instead of using public transport? Who made all these decisions? Were they made by brain processes? I don't think so. Were these decisions essential for survival purposes and therefore made by one or the other physiological processes of the body? I don't think so. All these decisions were taken *willfully* by Consciousness, although *it is the brain where the necessary and corresponding bodily processes take place to bring the decisions to a successful end.*

During certain spiritual and parapsychological experiences, a neurologist *may* detect an increase in activity in localized areas of the brain, but the question remains: Did the brain activity produce the spiritual experience, or did the spiritual experience activate the particular areas of the brain? My standpoint is that the spiritual experience is an act of Consciousness and it *may* cause an increase in brain activity. I say "may" because I am convinced that there are very profound spiritual experiences where the Consciousness of the person is detached from the body to the extent that no effect is produced on the brain.

An example that the operation of Consciousness is not rigorously affixed to the body is the phenomena of Near-Death Experience (NDE). An NDE takes place when you are unconscious, such as after a serious accident, or when you are under anesthesia undergoing a surgical procedure, or when you are in coma. Concisely, what happens is that you find yourself floating out of your body and traveling through a dark tunnel at the end of which is a bright light. When you reach the end of the tunnel, you may see a very beautiful landscape and hear celestial music. You may be greeted by angelical figures and by family members who died some time before. In a matter of seconds, your whole life will be shown and described to you with inclusion of the effect your acts had on other people. Finally, with your consensus a decision is reached on whether you will "stay on that side" or go back to your body. After retaking full control of your body, you may remember all the details of the experience. The experience itself may have many variances from one person to another, and so does the effect of the experience. Most NDEs are left with a profound spiritual feeling in their life. *Let me mention emphatically that NDE is not an illusion or delusion and is not the result of any medical malfunction in the body.* Studies have shown that 14 to 80 percent of people who have had a cardiac arrest have had an NDE. For more detailed information on NDE, please refer to the list at the end of this book.

Now, why would NDE serve as an indication that Consciousness is not inexorably attached to the brain? First, because most people having an NDE show a flat EEG—that is, the brain is not going through any activity at the moment of the experience. If the brain generates Consciousness, then how could it be totally inactive while *the conscious act* of NDE is taking place? Second, it is common that after recovering from unconsciousness most people have a brief cessation of memory due to the temporary inactivity of the brain. After an NDE, this is not the case. The person may refer to the experience right after recovering from unconsciousness. Third, if Consciousness was strictly a result of brain imprints, then anything you are conscious of must have been previously processed by your brain. However, there are circumstances where this is not the case. I will mention only two examples. One: a person who was born blind having an NDE would describe elaborate events the individual could, of course, never have seen before. Two: during an NDE, at the other end of the tunnel, a person was greeted by several people. Among them was a very kind man he had never known before. He was impressed by the love this man radiated. When he returned to normal consciousness, he related the NDE to his mother. She asked him to describe the man. His mother, who looked very distressed, then told him that he was born from a relationship she had before marrying her husband. She showed him a picture of his biological father, who had died shortly after his birth. There was a perfect match between the man he had seen in his NDE and the picture. NDEs would hover over their body for some time before or after returning from their experience, and when they recovered from their anesthesia or coma, they could tell what had been said and even thought by doctors and nurses in the room, and they could describe surgical instruments and medical procedures they had never seen or heard of before.

Further, there are uncountable anecdotes of people who have received messages from their dear ones at the moment of dying. There are also innumerable accounts of mediums that cannot just be discarded without a serious investigation. And finally I would like to mention earnest exploration in the field of telepathy, telekinesis, remote viewing, and healing, of which some can be explained only by the ever-pervading Consciousness. Of course there is also much deceit and folklore in these matters. I recommend further reading.

Out-of-Body Experience (OBE) is a somewhat similar experience to NDE. Here the subject's Consciousness floats out of the body, goes through walls and ceilings, and visits several places without any hindrances as to space. OBEs can be produced by will.

Another issue to be considered here is hypnosis. Hypnosis is a stage of high susceptibility to suggestion; in the normal awakened state, our brain operates in the beta stage, but under hypnosis it operates in the alpha or theta stage. In deep trance a subject may be given the suggestion (a belief) of not hearing certain sounds, and the person will not hear them, although the cerebral procedure corresponding to hearing takes place in the brain. Another example is the suggestion under hypnosis of not seeing a person standing in front of you, or seeing everybody in the room as naked. Again, the normal cerebral procedure corresponding to seeing takes place in the brain, but Consciousness, with the belief of not seeing implanted (temporarily), sees a totally different image. One last example: normally, if you touch the arm of a subject with a lit cigarette, a blister is created on where the person was burned. If the subject is under hypnosis and you touch the arm with a pencil but *suggest* that it was touched by a lit cigarette, *a blister will appear*. How can a blister appear when there was no lit cigarette and no heat? How can Consciousness override the normal messages of the brain? If Consciousness is an epiphenomenon of the brain, how can it be so much more powerful than the brain, how can it "fool" the brain? In all these cases it was Consciousness overriding and acting against the electrochemical processes in the brain.

What actually happens under hypnosis? The hypnotist gives a suggestion to his client. What is the suggestion in essence? It is a belief; a temporary belief is implanted in his Belief System and the Sub-Conscious, being enclosed in the vessel called body, will just follow orders to suit the Belief System via the life force called mind or soul. Once more we see the power of the Belief System; Consciousness, while attached to the body via the mind, can carry out and undergo only experiences that are in the Belief System of that particular person.

By the way, it is very important for the hypnotist to remove (by suggestion) the beliefs that under normal awakened condition can cause harm to a client.

There are other phenomena that are hard to explain if we insist that the brain must have previously and unconditionally processed all events taking place in the psyche. Take the work of *trustworthy* healers, mediums, and shamans; messages sent to family members by people about to die; appearances and messages from the spiritual world; and accounts of previous lives, reincarnation, and regression therapy. There are uncountable cases that merit serious study.

But let me state emphatically that I refuse all those TV programs, radio programs, and people who deal with card-reading, cold-reading, angelical healing, and so on, where you receive ambiguous messages with deceitful intentions.

Then there is the presence of Consciousness in animals, plants, and minerals, although in a somewhat reduced and less conspicuous degree. Migrating birds and schools of fish also exhibit a group Consciousness, and so do insects such as ants, termites, and bees. Flocks of more than a thousand birds can change direction in as fast as forty milliseconds as if they were one organism. Experiments with plants have shown **they react in several ways to emotions expressed by human beings**, and also minerals can react to these emotions **by changing their structure.**

I also want to refer to the morphogenetic resonance field. This is a Consciousness field in which an animal will copy the behavior of its kind although they are separated thousands of kilometers from each other. An example: a bird learns by chance a certain behavior, and other birds of its kind will also learn the behavior from the first one. After a certain number of birds (this amount is referred to as the critical mass) have learned the behavior, all birds of the same kind, thousands of kilometers away, will suddenly imitate the behavior without having had any contact with the bird or birds that first started the behavior. This field also affects humans; when a critical mass of people behaves in a certain way, the rest tend to follow suit. Experiments have been carried out where a group of citizens in a town meditated all at the same time, and it so happened that there was a decline in criminality in that town.

Consciousness and the Material World

But where does Consciousness come from? Consciousness is the highest degree, the ultimate degree of existence, and **it has always been there**. What good is it for matter to exist if there is no Consciousness to be aware of it? So, Consciousness must have existed before matter, and I would say that Consciousness created matter. Consciousness brought matter into existence because what is the purpose of Consciousness if there is nothing to be conscious about, and what is the purpose of matter if there is not something, like Consciousness, to be aware that it is there? We can still go a step further: isn't the whole material world an illusion created by Consciousness? Consciousness needed to experience itself, and to experience itself it created the material world. In quantum physics we know that the moment the physicist wants to detect a subatomic particle, only then does the subatomic particle pop into existence; before that it existed only as a probability. The moment the physicist is determined to find it, at that moment the probability wave collapses and the particle comes into existence.

Consciousness creates subatomic particles. Atoms consist of subatomic particles. Molecules consist of atoms. And the whole world around us consists of molecules. Isn't the world a creation by convenience? How could Consciousness become aware of its own existence? By creating the material world. Through the material world, Consciousness experiences Itself and becomes aware of Its own existence. Consciousness is intimately connected to matter. It manifests Itself through matter. It is because Consciousness is so entangled to matter that some scientists think it is an epiphenomenon of matter.

Some thirty-five thousand years ago, we humans were dormant consciously, and we felt we were one with the animal and plant world. Progressively we started awakening, and we then developed to a stage where we treated animals and plants as if we were superior to them, as if they were there to be exploited by us. We poison our rivers and seas, we cut down our forests, and we pollute our air. We make war and kill millions of our own kind. We value material belongings more than anything else. We have lost interest in the sharing of love. Now we are going back; we are going back inside, and we now pay more attention to spiritual practices.

Consciousness is **one**. There are no you and no me. Consciousness is so entangled to the body and confused by the Belief Systems, ego, habits, emotions, and desires that It created individualities; we became "you" and "me." **We reincarnate, not to acquire more and more wisdom—no, Consciousness is absolute wisdom. We reincarnate to become less and less ignorant, to cleanse ourselves from the ignorance of our Belief System. Our purpose in life is now to find our true nature, to return to our source, to become fully Conscious, to become aware that we are God, because God and Universal Consciousness are one.**

We are all entangled in the Universal Consciousness and, according to quantum physics, we will always be connected. You, as an individual Consciousness are everywhere in parallel worlds, and you can instantaneously communicate with an uncountable number of yous in the universe.

God is Absolute Consciousness. It permeates the whole universe. There is nothing more in the universe.

There is only Consciousness. **This Consciousness, being absolute, cannot experience Itself.** To experience Itself it needs a body, it needs a "you" and a "me," it needs "a subject" and an "object," it needs "outside" and "inside," it needs a "Belief System," it needs "emotions," it needs "feelings," it needs "a memory." So, in some way the Absolute Consciousness becomes each of us, and it is through us that it experiences the world, or rather, the illusion of a world. It looks as if Absolute Consciousness has divided itself to become each of us, but that is also an illusion. **So, God-Universal-Consciousness experiences the world through us. We are all God-Universal-Consciousness dressed in a body and in a Belief System that obscures our true being.** The Belief System is imprinted in the soul (life force) that envelops Consciousness. With each incarnation we get rid of more and more erroneous beliefs, and so more and more of the true nature of Consciousness is revealed. We go through this growth process until we become enlightened and the Consciousness is absorbed in the Universal-God-Consciousness. We lose our individuality, and we do not have to re-incarnate anymore. But, what exactly is Consciousness? We do not know. Who is "we"? Consciousness. Do "you" understand it now?

Let loose! Just "be"! "You" do not exist! "I" do not exist! Only Consciousness exists!

Chapter 6

A NEW WORLD

Albert Einstein once said, "The world is a dangerous place to be, not because of the people who are evil, but because of the people who don't do anything about it." We could say that less than 1 percent of the people are evil, and more than 99 percent are those who don't do anything about it. We lead apathetic lives; the 1 percent slaughter each other while we, the 99 percent, just look on. We do not protest against our governments; we do not question our religions. We feast, we consume, and we value materialism. In this last chapter of my book, I want to introduce you to some systems that might serve you for spiritual growth. I will be succinct; for further studies the reader may refer to the literature list at the end of this book or to the Internet.

The Power of Intention

Behind everything in the universe, there is a power called intention. According to the dictionary, intention is: "1) the act of determining upon some action or result; 2) the end or object intended." As I said in Chapter 1, there is intention behind every single act of creation in the universe. Every seed of every plant is impregnated by intention. Behind every spermatozoid, every ovum, and every molecule there is the power of intention. Intention is the drive in the universe to create, to manifest. It is a metaphysical force present continuously. Every billionth of a second, it is manifesting in the whole universe. It is boundlessly and endlessly abundant.

Intention is the force through which You-Consciousness-God can create whatever you want.

- **You know subconsciously how to create whatever you want, but because You-Consciousness are obscured by your Belief System, you seem to have forgotten. Let me just remind you of the procedures.**

1) **You should know for sure that this is going to work.** It is not a belief, it is not a dogma, and it is not some sort of ingenuity. You are the cocreator of the universe. If you don't believe, then forget it—it is not going to work.
2) **There must be kindness and love behind your intention.** Keep in mind the following: a) Whatever you give will come back to you; if you seek to harm, the pain of the harm will come back to you. You should always be kind and loving. b) You must be convinced that you deserve what you intend. The idea of not deserving is a religious belief. Discard it. We all deserve everything. c) Make sure you know clearly what you want. You don't have to get into minute details, but the general picture has to be clear and beyond doubt. d) Don't wish for a hundred material things. It will ultimately confuse and mislead you. Be simple, clear, and focused.

3) **There are no exact rules.** Nobody has written exact rules in the name of Universal Consciousness. One way to do it is to combine your thoughts with your feelings. Inhale deeply three to five times and then say, "I intend love to myself and the world. I intend peace to myself and the world. I intend health to myself and the world. I intend…(ask specifically what you want for yourself)." Feel that what you are asking for comes out of your heart. Finally say, "Thank you, Universe." You thank the universe because the universe is cocreating with you. Focus! When you express your intentions, imagine the message spreading through the whole universe. Repeat your intentions seven times or any number of times that is your favorite number. Repeat step 3 five or seven times a day. Feel that you are doing an exercise that really works. There are no strict rules of how the exercise should be done. The secret is the sincerity of your intention, the pureness of thought, and the effective force of the intention itself. **You may forget the details I have mentioned here; as long as you are sincere and rational and you proceed with your intuition, it will work. There are no rules written in the Universe.**
4) **Act as if your intention has been accomplished and detach from step 3.** Do not walk all the time around thinking of your intentions. Let go! Feel satisfaction and gratitude in you and act as if your intentions have been realized. If you asked for health, feel healthy; if you asked for prosperity, feel prosperous; feel whatever you ask for. Feeling radiates from your heart. Be at peace!

5) **Be patient. It may take some time for the right conditions to come together in order to realize your intention.** Be grateful, and be at peace; practice kindness, love, and forgiveness. There is abundance in the universe. It is at our reach, and we all deserve it. Feel that your center of attention is in your ninth chakra (1.2 meter above your head), and whenever the slightest thought of doubt arises say, "Intention, intention, intention." Feel peace and love for the whole world; the whole world deserves peace and love.

For more information, visit the website of Institute of HeartMath.

Mindfulness

Live in the now. The past is a now already gone, and the future is a now yet to come. Almost all our problems are in the past and the future. We suffer thinking of what we could have accomplished in the past but didn't. We suffer thinking of what we would like to accomplish in the future but do not have the resources to do. The past is gone, and the future still has to come. But every time the future comes, we call it "now," and every time "now" has gone, we call it past. Actually, even "now" does not exist because if the past and the future do not exist, then "now" cannot exist because now is the dividing line between past and future. But for the sake of convenience, we will keep using the word *now*.

Our mind is constantly flowing between "past" and "future." We worry the whole time. We are busy trying to solve problems continually, and we are not aware that the actual problem is in the going "back and forth" of our mind. We have no peace of mind. That is the basic problem. We do not concentrate in what we are doing in this precise moment. To solve this problem, we have to live with mindfulness—that is, we have to fully concentrate on the act we are busy with. Are you eating? Concentrate; feel the taste of the food in your mouth. Is it too salty? Is the taste just right? Are you washing the dishes? Concentrate. You may wonder how the soap dissolves the grease. When you are painting, concentrate. How does the paint cover the wall? For every act, concentrate, concentrate, concentrate. If you are continually concentrating on what you are doing, you will notice that **you have no problems**.

You may think that this way of living is going to drive you crazy, but it is not so! On the contrary, not living this way is driving you crazy! It is the going back and forth of your mind that will deplete your energy. Life is taking place right now, in this billionth of a second, but you are living in the nonexistent past or in the nonexistent future, and that is driving you crazy.

A step further from mindfulness is awareness. When something happens to you, be aware of what it is that happens. Say you suddenly felt anger. Stop. Think. Become aware of what exactly made you angry. "Oh, it was the words my friend said some minutes ago." OK, what belief did I attach to the words to choose becoming angry? I attached this…belief. OK, I decide at this moment that I will discard this belief. This belief has been causing me a lot of trouble, and I do not want that. *I have just made more progress in the control over my Belief System!"*

Buddhism

Buddhism is not a religion. It is a way of living—although some people have made a religion out of Buddhism. The tenets of Buddhism are made clear in the Four Noble Truths and the Noble Eightfold Path. I recommend you to put aside religion and instead live according to the tenets of Buddhism. You do not have to visit any temple, and you do not have to look up to any guru. You just live a simple, mindful life. As much as you are able, you can be at peace, live with compassion, and practice kindness to all human beings, animals, and plants.

The Four Noble Truths
1) **There is suffering in life.** This means life includes feeling pain, getting old, becoming sick, and ultimately dying. You also have psychological suffering, loneliness, fear, disappointment, and anger. This is not a matter of pessimism—it is realistic, and we will also learn how to avoid suffering.
2) **Suffering is caused by craving and aversion.** We suffer because we expect others to live according to our expectations. We want others to like us. We always want more and more possessions. We are never satisfied. We live with greed and anger. We are never at peace.
3) **Suffering can be overcome and happiness can be attained.** If we give up craving, and if we live each day with mindfulness and awareness, then we can attain peace.
4) **Suffering can be stopped if we follow The Eightfold Path.**

The Eightfold Path
1) **Right view.** Suffering enters our life through our desires. Letting go of desires will bring peace, and we are able to attain Right View. To look at the world the right way is to look with peace, with kindness, with love.

2) **Right thought.** The world is the fruit of our thoughts. Avoid the thoughts that are born from craving. Choose for reasonable, intelligent thoughts.
3) **Right speech.** Abstain from lies, and avoid harsh and unproductive speech.
4) **Right action.** Avoid exploitation of yourself and others. Let your actions conduct to the happiness of yourself and of others around you. Remember, eventually all you do comes back to you in one way or another.
5) **Right livelihood.** Practice peace and love. Do not cause harm to human beings, animals, plants, or nature in general.

6) **Right effort.** Your path to liberation must be firm and executed with right effort.
7) **Right mindfulness.** Be aware of your body, your feelings, your mind, and your thoughts.
8) **Right concentration.** Continue on the path for always developing your skills. Be mindful and aware all the time, and it will be easy to practice Buddhism.

Always walk around as if your aware center is in your ninth chakra.

Why Do People Pray?
The following are some of the reasons why people pray:

People may pray because they are afraid of what comes hereafter. They may pray and ask god to grant them a place in heaven. Well, you should understand that there is no such place as heaven. The Christians pray for a place in heaven, the Muslims do the same, and the

Hindus also do it. Every religion does it. They all have different beliefs; do they have the same heaven? Are there different heavens? Which is the real one? None of them! Heaven is on earth; it is the wonderful feeling you get when you live with thoughts of peace and love for the whole planet, for the whole universe. Hell is the disturbed mind with which you live when you are constantly craving, when you are angry, or whenever you have ill feelings. The truth is, Consciousness keeps on going forever. You will notice it immediately after the so-called death. Dying can be a peaceful process if you just let loose and go toward the light.

People may pray when they are sick or when their loved ones are sick. You can alleviate or cure yourself and others from sickness. Sit down in a chair with your back straight. Now visualize the sick person. Now imagine yourself rising from your body and visiting the other person in the form of a white light. Surround the stressed person completely in the white light and express the very best of your intentions to help him or her. Express peace and love. Do not be specific as to the kind of sickness; just express the intention to help. Stay there for a few minutes. The healing is in your intention. Do the same with yourself.

People may pray to ask a favor. I recommend you use instead the force of intention.

And finally, you may pray. Express your prayer to the Universal God-Consciousness (which is ultimately yourself). The bottom line is this: **you can never do it wrong.** If your intentions are sincere, if they are pure, then it is always good and it might and most probably will work.**Your good intentions always work!Your intentions of peace and love are the intentions of Universal-God-Consciousness!**

A New World Order

I propose a new world order that should include the following:We abandon the belief in punishment and reward by "god". The "sins" you make are lessons from which you learn to improve your life. There are no sins; there are only lessons.We abandon the belief in a heaven and a hell. When we leave this world, we stay in another realm of Consciousness. Eventually we will reincarnate in this world, where we keep on making spiritual progress (spiritual evolution) until we reach a moment where we are absorbed fully in It, Consciousness-God; we become enlightened. I will elaborate on reincarnation in another book.We abandon all dogmas and beliefs related to so-called special powers endowed by god to men, such as the idea that the pope is the representative on earth of god and Jesus, that our sins are forgiven in confession, that the pope is infallible, that we go to heaven by killing infidels in the name of Allah, and so on.We abandon patriotism. The world itself has no borders. All countries are convenient limits set by historical agreements and wars. Our governments use patriotism to make us go to war against our brothers in other countries. **We are all citizens of the world.** All major decisions by our governments need the approval of the people.We disapprove of all weapons kept by our government. All weapons should be destroyed. All armies should be dissolved. Think of peace.We are all entitled to food, education, health care, and proper housing.We should not accept any social differences between men and women, nor should we discriminate people by race, religion, or nationalities. We should revolt against all dictators, all corrupted governments, and all corrupted organizations.We should revolt against all religions whose sole purpose is to keep us ignorant by impregnating us with fearful and distorted beliefs. Governments around the world and all of us should take a stance and protest against child labor, child prostitution, and war children, as in Africa, India and Asia.

- We should abolish all death penalties.

In this New World Order, everyone should meditate three times a day for at least twenty minutes. During this time we free our minds from all thoughts; we are at peace. A resonance field will form with billions of people all over the world with the same thought of peace and love. This will ultimately bring peace in the world.

I know that all this sounds like Utopia—**but it is not.** We have been doubting, we have been postponing, we have been turning our backs, and centuries have gone by. Now it is time for civilized people to take up their responsibility. We have to start a spiritual revolution, without arms. We must take action, without killing each other. We must embrace, we must share, and we must love. At this moment we are destroying our planet; we are extinguishing species after species of animals, we are fouling our rivers, lakes, and seas; and we are waging wars with thousands and millions of casualties. People are dying every second from hunger and lack of water. Corruption is becoming widespread in politics and business. Governments are spending $ 4 billion in war every day while at the same time seventy thousand human beings are dying every day because they do not have enough food. **We must protest now!** How and when will we put an end to all this? Are we waiting for a miracle? Miracles do not exist. If we begin now, and I mean NOW, **there will come a change**—if not over one year then over five years—but we should start **NOW**.

Dear reader of this book: I don't know your name. I do not need to know your name. But I know this much: it is your responsibility to change this world for the better. You have to start now. It is your planet, **your planet**. If you destroy it, you destroy yourself. So, sit down for a few minutes every day and think of peace, of love; we will form together a resonance field and we will succeed. I can assure you: there will be peace, there will be love! Contact me and share your opinion with me; I cannot do it alone, **I need you!**

God-Consciousness is all there is; we are God-Consciousness, and God-Consciousness is us. May peace and love be with you.

hadsysimon@gmail.com

FURTHER READING

There is nothing I can recommend more than reading. By reading, you acquire knowledge that may improve your daily life experiences and also contribute to a better world. I offer you here a list of the books I have read in the past fifteen years. There are thousands more; you can decide for yourself what appeals most to you

On Consciousness, Quantum Mechanics, God
Aczel, Amir—*Entanglement.*
Al-Khalili, Jim—*Quantum: A Guide for the Perplexed.*
Bohm, David and Peat, David—*Science, Order, and Creativity.*
Davies, Paul—*God and the New Physics.*
Davies, Paul— *The Mind of God.*
Elgin, Duane—*The Living Universe: Where Are We? Who Are We? Where Are We Going?*
Epstein, Lewis Carroll—*Relativity Visualized.*
Goswami, Amit—*Physics of the Soul: The Quantum Book of Living, Dying, Reincarnation, and Immortality.*
Greene, Brian—*The Elegant Universe.*
Grof, Stanislav—*The Ultimate Journey: Consciousness and the Mystery of Death.*
Haisch, Bernard—*The Purpose-Guided Universe: Believing in Einstein, Darwin, and God.*

Herbert, Nick—*Elemental Mind: Human Consciousness and the New Physics.*
Lanza, Robert—*Biocentrism: How Life and Consciousness Are the Keys to Understanding the True Nature of the Universe.*
Laszlo, Ervin—*The Connectivity Hypothesis: Foundations of an Integral Science of Quantum, Cosmos, Life, and Consciousness.*
Malin, Shimon—*Nature Loves to Hide: Quantum Physics and the Nature of Reality, a Western Perspective.*
Marshall, Ian and Zohar, Danah—*Who's Afraid of Schrodinger's Cat? An A-to-Z Guide to All the New Science Ideas You Need to Keep Up with the New Thinking*
Kaku, Michio—*Hyperspace: A Scientific Odyssey Through Parallel Universes, Time Warps, and the 10th Dimension.*
Radin, Dean—*The Physics of Consciousness.*
Rosenblum, Bruce and Kuttner, Fred—*Quantum Enigma: Physics Encounters Consciousness.*
Russell, Peter—*From Science to God: A Physicist's Journey into the Mystery of Consciousness.*
Smoley, Richard—*The Dice Game of Shiva: How Consciousness Creates the Universe.*
Talbot, Michael—*Beyond the Quantum.*
Tiller, William—*Science and Human Transformation: Subtle Energies, Intentionality and Consciouness.* Toben, Bob—*Space-Time and Beyond.*
Walker, Evan Harris—*The Physics of Consciousness: The Quantum Mind and the Meaning of Life.*
Watson, Lyall—*Dark Nature: Natural History of Evil.*
Weinberg, Steven—*Dreams of a Final Theory: The Scientist's Search for the Ultimate
Laws of Nature.*
Wilber, Ken—*The Spectrum of Consciousness.*

Wolf, Fred Alan—*Star Wave: Mind, Consciousness, and Quantum Physics.*
Wolf, Fred Alan—*The Spiritual Universe: One Physicist's Vision of Spirit, Soul, Matter, and Self.*
Wolf, Fred Alan—*Taking the Quantum Leap: The New Physics for Nonscientists.*
Zeilinger, Anton—*Toeval!* (Dutch).

Universe, Mathematics, Physics

Barbour, Julian—*The End of Time.*
Briggs, John and Peat, David—*Looking Glass Universe: The Emerging Science of Wholeness.*
Davies, Paul and Gribbin, John—*The Matter Myth: Dramatic Discoveries that Challenge Our Understanding of Physical Reality.*
Guillen, Michael—*Five Equations That Changed the World: The Power and Poetry of Mathematics.*
Hawking, Stephen—*The Universe in a Nutshell.*
Kahan, Gerald—*E=mc2: Picture Book of Relativity.*
Krauss, Lawrence—*A Universe from Nothing. Why There Is Something Rather Than Nothing.*
McTaggart, Lynne—*The Field: The Quest for the Secret Force of the Universe.*
Oldfield, Harry and Coghill, Roger—*The Dark Side of the Brain: Major Discoveries in the Use of Kirlian Photography and Electrocrystal Therapy.*
Russell, Peter—*The White Hole in Time.*
Schwartz, Gary and Russek, Linda—*The Living Energy Universe.*
Siegfried, Tom—*Strange matters: Undiscovered Ideas at the Frontiers of Space and Time.*
Tolle, Eckhart—*The Power of Now: A Guide to Spiritual Enlightenment.*

Tolle, Eckhart—*A New Earth: Awakening to Your Life's Purpose.*

Reality, Belief System

Adams, James—*Conceptual Blockbusting: A Guide to Better Ideas*
Watzlawick, Paul—*The Invented Reality: How Do We Know What We Believe We Know?*
Watzlawick, Paul—Ultra-Solutions: How to Fail Most Successfully.
Watzlawick, Paul and Weakland, John and Fisch, Richard—*Change: Principles of Problem Formation and Problem Resolution.*
Poe, Rahasya—*To Believe or Not to Believe: The Social and Neurological
Consequences of Belief Systems.*

Kabbalah, Buddhism

Berg, Philip—*To the Power of One.*
Cooper, David—*God Is a Verb: Kabbalah and the Practice of Mystical Judaism.*
Khema, Ayya—*Being Nobody, Going Nowhere: Meditations on the Buddhist Path.*
Parsons, Tony—*The Open Secret.*

Philosophy, Psychology, Biology, Spirituality

Aaron, David—*The Secret Life of God: Discovering the Divine within You.*
Abram, David—*The Spell of the* Sensuous: *Perception and Language in a More-Than-Human World.*
Andersen, Uell—*Three Magic Words.*
Armstrong, Karen—*A History of God.*
Aufenanger, Jörg—*Beknopte Inleiding in de Filosofie* (Dutch).

Bateson, Gregory—*Mind and Nature: A Necessary Unity (Advances in Systems Theory, Complexity, and the Human Sciences).*
Brunton, Paul—*The Wisdom of the Overself.*
Campbell, Joseph—*Myths to Live By.*
Capra, Fritjof—*The Tao of Physics: An Exploration of the Parallels Between Modern Physics and Eastern Mysticism.*
Cope, Stephen—*Yoga and the Quest for the True Self.*
Craig, Edward—*Philosophy, a Very Short Introduction.*
Damasio, Antonio—*The Feeling of What Happens: Body and Emotion in the Making of Consciousness.*
Dawkins, Richard—*The Selfish Gene.*
De Leander, Jan—*Het Hard van de Duisternis* (Dutch).
De Quincey, Christian—*Consciousness from Zombies to Angels: The Shadow and the Light of Knowing Who You Are.*
De Quincey, Christian—*Radical Nature: Rediscovering the Soul of Matter.*
Dyer, Wayne—*Getting in the Gap: Making Conscious Contact with God Through Meditation.*
Fenner, Peter—*Reasoning into Reality: A System Cybernetics Model and Therapeutic Interpretation of Buddhist Middle Path Analysis.*
Friedman, Norman—*Bridging Science and Spirit: Common Elements in David Bohm's Physics, the Perennial Philosophy and Seth.*
Goddard, Neville—*Power of Awareness.*
Goddard, Neville—*The Neville Reader: A Collection of Spiritual Writings and Thoughts on Your Inner Power to Create an Abundant Life.*
Goswami, Amit—*The Self-Aware Universe: How Consciousness Creates the Material World.*
Grof, Stanislav and Grof, Christina—*Spiritual Emergency: When Personal Transformation Becomes a Crisis.*

Grof, Stanislav—*The Adventure of Self-Discovery: Dimensions of Consciousness and New Perspectives in Psychotherapy and Inner Exploration.*
Hanson, Rick—*Buddha's Brain: The Practical Neuroscience of Happiness, Love, and Wisdom.*
Haisch, Bernard—*The God Theory: Universes, Zero-Point Fields, and What's Behind It All.*
Hitchens, Christopher—*God Is Not Great: How Religion Poisons Everything.*Jawer, Michael, Micozzi, Marc and Dossey, Larry—*The Spiritual Anatomy of Emotion: How Feelings Link the Brain, the Body, and the Sixth Sense.*
Keleman, Stanley—*Your Body speaks its Mind.*
Kinslow, Frank—*Quantum Healing in het dagelijks leven* (Dutch).
Kinslow, Frank—*Quantum Healing; het geheim van spontane genezing* (Dutch).
Kornfield, Jack—*A Path with Heart: A Guide Through the Perils and Promises of Spiritual Life.*
Kushner, Harold—*Who Needs God.*
Laszlo, Ervin—*Quantum Shift in the Global Brain: How the New Scientific Reality Can Change Us and Our World.*
Laszlo, Ervin—*Science and the Re-Enchantment of the Cosmos: The Rise of the Integral Vision of Reality.*
Laszlo, Ervin—*Science and the Akashic Field: An Integral Theory of Everything.*
LeDoux, Joseph—*The Emotional Brain: The Mysterious Underpinnings of Emotional Life.*
Levine Hoberman, Barbara—*Your Body Believes Every Word You Say: The Language of the Body/Mind.*
Levine, Peter—*Walking the Tiger: Healing Trauma.*
Margenau, Henry—*The Miracle of Existence.*
McDougall, Joyce—*Theaters of the Body: A Psychoanalytic Approach to Psychosomatic Illness.*
Minsky, Marvin—*The Society of Mind.*

Moody, A. Raymond—*Reunions: Visionary Encounters with Departed Loved Ones.*
Nathanson, Donald—*Shame and Pride: Affect, Sex, and the Birth of the Self.*
Neckebrouck, Valeer—*Beelden van de sjamaan* (Dutch).
Newton, Michael—*Destiny of Souls: New Case Studies of Life between Lives.*
Peacocke, Arthur R.—*Van DNA tot God* (Dutch).
Petrella, Riccardo—*Menselijk Verlangen* (Dutch).
Polkinghorne, John—*Quarks, Chaos en Christendom* (Dutch).
Radin, Dean—*Entangled Minds: Extrasensory Experiences in a Quantum Reality.*
Ralston, Peter—*The Book of Not Knowing: Exploring the True Nature of Self, Mind, and Consciousness.*
Raub, John Jacob—*Who Told You That You Were Naked?: Freedom From Judgement, Guilt and Fear of Punishment*
Rothschild, Babette—*The Body Remembers: The Psychophysiology of Trauma and Trauma Treatment.*
Rozemond, Klaas—*Filosofie Voor de Zwijnen* (Dutch).
Saratoga and Telstar—*The Final Elimination of the Source of Fear.*
Savater, Fernando—*Las Preguntas de la Vida* (Spanish).
Schilthuizen, Menno—*Het Mysterie der Mysteriën* (Dutch).
Schoenewolf, Gerald—*The Art of Hating.*
Seligman, Martin—*Authentic happiness: Using the New Positive Psychology to Realize Your Potential for Lasting Fulfillment.*
Sheldrake, Rupert—*A New Science of Life: The Hypothesis of Morphic Resonance.*
Stephen, Law—*Filosofische Fitness* (Dutch).
Steven, Sadleir—*The Theory of Existence & the Science of Consciousness.*
Steven, Sadleir—*Self-Realization.*

Stone, Joshua David—*Soul Psychology: How to Clear Negative Emotions and Spiritualize Your Life.*
Talbot, Michael—*The Holographic Universe: The Revolutionary Theory of Reality.*
Tart, Charles—*The End of Materialism: How Evidence of the Paranormal Is Bringing Science and Spirit Together.*
Todorov, Tzvetan—*Herinneringen aan het Kwaad, Bekoring van het Goede* (Dutch).
van Bendegem, Jean Paul—*Logica* (Dutch).
van Lommel, Pim—*Eindeloos Bewustzijn* (Dutch).
van Peursen, C.A.—*Filosofische Oriëntatie* (Dutch).
Warners, Ilse—*Terug naar de Oorsprong* (Dutch).
Warburton, Nigel—*Philosophy, the Basics.*
Wilber, Ken—*The Atman Project: A Transpersonal View of Human Development.*
Wilber, Ken (Edited)—*Quantum Questions.*
Wilber, Ken—*The Essential Ken Wilber.*
Zukav, Gary—*The Dancing Wu Li Masters.*
Zukav, Gary—*The Seat of the Soul.*

The Roman Catholic Church
Christopher, Hitchens—*God Is Not Great: How Religion Poisons Everything.*
Truyman, André—*Schijn van Heiligheid; Benedictus XVI en Johannes Paulus II* (Dutch).
van Lochem, Kitty—*Omvallende Dogma's* (Dutch).
Woodrow, Ralph Edward—*Babylon Mystery Religion, Ancient and Modern.*
Yallop, David—*In God's Name: An Investigation into the Murder of Pope John Paul I.*
Yallop, David—*The Power and the Glory: Inside the Dark Heart of Pope John Paul II's Vatican.*

General Interest
Bailey, Darryl—*Dismantling the Fantasy.*

Bennett, Deborah—*Logic Made Easy: How to Know When Language Deceives You.*
Braden, Gregg—*Awakening to Zero Point.*
Braden, Gregg—*The Divine Matrix: Bridging Time, Space, Miracles, and Belief.*
Bourne, Edmund J.—*Global Shift: How a New Worldview Is Transforming Humanity.*
Buscaglia, Leo—*Love: What Life Is All About.*
Campbell, Jeremy—*Grammatical Man: Information, Entropy, Language and Life.*
Capra, Fritjof—*The Web of Life: A New Scientific Understanding of Living Systems.*
De Mello, Anthony—*One Minute Wisdom.*
Dohmen, Joep (Edited)—*Over Levenskunst.* (Dutch)
Dyer, Wayne—*The Power of Intention.*
Emoto, Masaru—*Water weet het Antwoord* (Dutch).
Erbe, Peter—*God I Am: From Tragic to Magic.*
Fischer, Ernst Peter (Edited)—*Einstein, Hawking, Singh & Co.*
Goldacre, Ben—*Bad Science: Quacks, Hacks, and Big Pharma Flacks.*
Goode, Greg—*Standing as Awareness.*
Grant, Anthony and Greene, Jane—*Coach Yourself.*
Gross, Eric—*Liberation from the Lie: Cutting the Roots of Fear Once and for All.*
Hawkins, David—*Power Versus Force: The Hidden Determinants of Human Behavior.*
Hodges, Wilfrid—*Logic.*
Khan, Hazrat Inayat—*The Mysticism of Sound and Music.*
Krishnamurti, J.—*The First and Last Freedom.*
Lakoff, George and Johnson, Mark—*Metaphors We Live By.*
MacLean, Kenneth J. M.—*The Vibrational Universe: Harnessing the Power of Thought to Consciously Create Your Life.*

McTaggart, Lynne—*The Intention Experiment: Using Your Thoughts to Change Your Life and the World.*
Monroe, Robert—*Journeys Out of the Body.*
Monroe, Robert—*Far Journeys.*
Monroe, Robert—*Ultimate Journey.*
Moody, Raymond—*The Last Laugh: A New Philosophy of Near-Death Experiences, Apparitions, and the Paranormal.*
Pearl, Eric—*The Reconnection.*
Pollan, Michael—*In Defense of Food: An Eater's Manifesto.*
Roberts, Jane—*Seth Speaks: The Eternal Validity of the Soul.*
Roberts, Jane—*The Seth Material.*
Rucker, Rudy—*The Fourth Dimension.*
Ruiz, Miguel—*The Four Agreements: A Practical Guide to Personal Freedom.*
Singer, Michael—*The Untethered Soul: The Journey Beyond Yourself.*
Schlitz, Marilyn M., et al.—*Living Deeply: The Art and Science of Transformation in Everyday Life.*
Schmid, Wilhelm—*Handboek voor de Levenskunst.* (Dutch)
Shermer, *Michael*—*How We Believe: Science, Skepticism, and the Search for God.*
Stappers, J. G.—*Massacommunicatie; een inleiding.* (Dutch).
Storr, Anthony—*Music and the Mind.*
Taylor, Eldon—*Mind Programming: From Persuasion and Brainwashing, to Self-Help and Practical Metaphysics.*
Taylor, Eldon—*What Does That Mean? Exploring Mind, Meaning, and Mysteries.*
Tompkins, Peter and Bird, Christopher—*The Secret Life of Plants: A Fascinating Account of the Physical, Emotional, and Spiritual Relations between Plants and Man.*
van den Berg, Natasha and Koers, Sophie—*Praktisch Idealisme.* (Dutch).
van Raak, Ronald—*Oud Licht op Nieuwe Zaken.* (Dutch).

Villoldo, Alberto—*The Four Insights: Wisdom, Power, and Grace of the Earthkeepers.*
Walsch, Neale Donald—*Tomorrow's God: Our Greatest Spiritual Challenge.*
Wolf, Fred Alan—*Mind into Matter: A New Alchemy of Science and Spirit.*

Politics, Economics

Albright, Madeleine—*The Mighty and the Almighty: Reflections on America, God, and World Affairs.*
Galtung, Johan—*The Fall of the US Empire—and Then What?*
Hertz, Noreena—*The Silent Takeover: Global Capitalism and the Death of Democracy.*
Knoops, Geert-Jan—*Blufpoker (International Justice),* (Dutch).
Pearce, Joseph—*Small Is Still Beautiful: Economics as if Families Mattered.*
Zaragoza, Federico Mayor—*Delito de Silencio,* (Spanish).

Hypnotherapy, NLP, Regression

Anderson, Jill—*Thinking, Changing, Rearranging: Improving Self-Esteem in Young People.*
Andreas, Steve—*Virginia Satir: The patterns of Her Magic.*
Araoz, Daniel—*The New Hypnosis.*
Bandler, Richard—*Magic in Action.*
Bandler, Richard and Grinder, John—*Reframing: Neuro-Linguistic Programming and the Transformation of Meaning.*
Bandler, Richard and Grinder, John—*Trance-formations: Neuro-Linguistic Programming and the Structure of Hypnosis.*
Bandler, Richard and Grinder, John—*The Structure of Magic* (two volumes).
Bandler, Richard and Grinder, John—*Frogs into Princes.*
Bandler, Richard—*Using Your Brain for a Change.*

Bandler, Richard and MacDonald, Will—*An Insider's Guide to Sub-Modalities.*
Barber, Joseph, et al.—*Hypnosis and Suggestion in the Treatment of Pain: A Clinical Guide.*
Blake Lucas, Winafred—*Regression Therapy: A Handbook for Professionals* (two volumes).
Boas, Phill—*An NLP Workbook, Advanced Techniques.*
Cladder, J. M.—*Hypnose als Hulpmiddel bij Psycho-Therapie.* (Dutch).
Chesworth, Michael—*Putting on the Brakes: Young People's Guide to Understanding Attention Deficit Hyperactivity Disorder.*
Gordon, David—*Therapeutic Metaphors: Helping Others through the Looking Glass.*
Hansen, P. T.—*Hypnose in de Praktijk.* (Dutch).
Haley, Jay—*Uncommon Therapy: The Psychiatric Techniques of Milton H. Erickson, M.D.*
Havens, Ronald and Walters, Catherine—*Hypnotherapy Scripts.*
Hudson O'Hanlon, William—*Taproots.*
Kappas, John—*Professional Hypnotism Manual: Introducing Physical and Emotional Suggestibility and Sexuality.*
Lankton, Steve—*Practical Magic: A Translation of Basic Neuro-Linguistic Programming into Clinical Psychotherapy.*
Lankton, Carol and Lankton, Steve—*Tales of Enchantment: Goal-Oriented Metaphors for Adults.*
Lecron, Leslie—*Self-Hypnotism: The Technique and Its Use in Daily Living.*
Lewis, Byron and Pucelik, Frank—*Magic of NLP Demystified: A Pragmatic Guide to Communication & Change.*
Lovern, John—*Pathways to Reality: Erickson-Inspired Treatment Approaches to Chemical Dependency.*

Moine, Donald and Lloyd, Kenneth—*Unlimited Selling Power: How to Master Hypnotic Selling Skills.*
O'Connor, Joseph and Seymour, John—*Introducing Neuro-Linguistic Programming: Psychological Skills for Understanding and Influencing People.*
Petrie, Sidney and Stone, Robert—*Hypno Cybernetics: Helping Yourself to a Rich, New Life.*
Rossi, Ernest and Cheek, David—*Mind-Body Therapy: Methods of Ideodynamic Healing in Hypnosis.*
Sommer, Bobbe—*Psycho-Cybernetics 2000.*
Stokvis, Berthold—*Hypnose in de Geneeskunde Praktijk.* (Dutch).
Yapko, Michael—*Trancework: An Introduction to the Practice of Clinical Hypnosis.*

Printed in Great Britain
by Amazon